"If you long for life-sharing friendshi
media relationships and a lack of ir
Wier skillfully weaves personal stories with biblical
abundance of action steps that will provide all the tools you need to develop lasting friendships. I especially benefited from her list of questions that help relationships to go deeper. Read this book yourself and then invite a group of women to go through the chapters together. I know you'll not only get wise instruction—you'll make lifetime friends!"

—Carol Kent, speaker and author of *Becoming a Woman of Influence*

"*This book. Oh my!* I was hooked from the very first sentence. Kim has a gift for weaving relatable and often hilarious stories with gentle Bible truths that guide us toward God's plan for relationships. *The Art of Friendship* reminds me why my friends are a gift—and how to treasure them well."

—Becky Kopitzke, author, speaker, writing coach

"Blending practical tips with biblical insight, Kim Wier paints a compelling portrait of the complexities of friendship, and the longing for community that stirs deep within our souls. Honest, relatable, and truth-filled, *The Art of Friendship* will inspire you to seek, pursue, and grow in authentic relationships."

—Amanda Barratt, author of *My Dearest Dietrich: A Novel of Dietrich Bonhoeffer's Lost Love*

"In a world dominated by shallow social media relationships, Kim Wier reminds us how biblical friendship is essential for life and joy, beautifully modeled by Christ. Using honest stories from her life and Scripture, Kim will take you by the hand and guide you to discover the true meaning of friendship."

—Kate Battistelli, author of *The God Dare*

"We are in an era where we are more connected than ever before, but the practice of friendship—the art of it, as Kim so beautifully writes—is becoming a lost expression. Kim gives us fresh perspective on what true connection and community look like, and she helps us understand God's purpose beyond ourselves for friendship, along with tangible ways we can develop new friendships and nurture old ones."

—Julie Lyles Carr, bestselling author of *Raising an Original* and *Footnotes*, pastor of LifeWomen Women's Ministry, host of *The Modern Motherhood* podcast

"Kim Wier has her thumb on the pulse of women's hopes, insecurities, and desires, illuminating issues that wear us down, build us up, wound, and heal. Contained within are the beautiful truths that God sees His daughters in all their beauty and delights in connecting them with each other."

—Kristen Heitzmann, bestselling author

"You would be hard-pressed to find much agreement between diverse thinkers such as noted Christian C. S. Lewis and ardent atheist Frederick Nietzsche. Yet they both agree that friendship should be our grandest pursuit. I can't think of a better guide in this crucial pursuit than Kim Wier."

—Tim Muehlhoff, professor of communication, Biola University

"In a world of online relationships falling woefully short of meeting our God-given need to connect, Kim Wier's wise thoughts on how to experience true friendship ground this wise and timely tutorial. And her wit—it's just icing on the cake! Kudos, Kim!"

—Shellie Rushing Tomlinson, author of the storytelling cookbook *Hungry Is a Mighty Fine Sauce*

"I had only read a few paragraphs of *The Art of Friendship* and I felt I was reading my story. There was an immediate heart and soul connection with Kim. Kim's words soothed aches that I didn't know I had stuffed way down deep. She speaks words of truth and hope, and I know I'd love to sit across the table from her and share a cup of coffee and slice of pie. I believe you would too."

—Tara Royer Steele, author, founder of Royers Pie Haven and graceupongracegirl.com

"Once again, I was shy and awkward with a tray of food I was too anxious to eat, wondering if someone would have a seat for me at the table. In *The Art of Friendship*, Kim Wier shows us a glimpse into her discovery of finding friendship at a young age and realizing the beauty of the friendship we often let slip away in the name of busyness and adulthood. You and I crave meaningful connection and friendship that fuels our souls; this book is your new BFF guidebook."

—Jennifer Renee Watson, author of *Freedom!: The Gutsy Pursuit of Breakthrough and the Life Beyond It*, and cohost of the *More Than Small Talk* podcast

"In a social media culture of taps, swipes, and likes, it's easy to wrongly assume that connecting with 'friends' all day long on a screen is actually friendship. In *The Art of Friendship*, Kim Wier taps in to the hows—and how not to's—of having up close, authentic relationships in a biblical and powerful, yet refreshingly practical way. Consider it your go-to guide for finding and maintaining healthy friendships, and also for knowing how to spot one that is not."

—Karen Ehman, *New York Times* bestselling author of *Keep It Shut: What to Say, How to Say It, and When to Say Nothing at All*

"Kim Wier has a way with words: She's funny, inspiring, heartfelt, and true. She has set her sights on raising the act of friendship to the level of art. If you've been feeling like your friendships are lackluster, less-than-intimate, or completely AWOL, let Kim remind you to pick up your paints and pallets and change the picture of your life."

—Anita Renfroe, comedian and author

THE *Art of* FRIENDSHIP

THE *Art of* FRIENDSHIP

Creating and Keeping Relationships that Matter

KIM WIER

BETHANYHOUSE
a division of Baker Publishing Group
Minneapolis, Minnesota

Published by Bethany House Publishers
11400 Hampshire Avenue South
Bloomington, Minnesota 55438
www.bethanyhouse.com

Bethany House Publishers is a division of
Baker Publishing Group, Grand Rapids, Michigan

Printed in the United States of America

ISBN 978-0-7642-3443-9

Library of Congress Control Number: 2019949895

Cover design by Emily Weigel
Cover photography by Jacob Lund

Author represented by The Gates Group

20 21 22 23 24 25 26 7 6 5 4 3 2 1

For Tony.

Every place I go and everything I do
and everyone I reach is your doing too.
In the words of e.e. cummings,
"I carry your heart with me . . . I am never without it."

Contents

1

Where's the BFF?

I recall the exact day I discovered my dog had more committed friendships than I had. I found myself in midlife and bereft of girlfriends, and I hadn't realized how deficient my relationships were.

For the past twenty years, I have written a faith-based humor column for our local newspaper. The column chronicles the ups, downs, joys, and challenges of life in rural Texas—and specifically in the life of the Wier family. Along with storytelling, I share a spiritual insight, a lesson of faith, or a word of encouragement. Through the years the readers have watched my kids grow up, laughed at their mischief (and mine), and generally enjoyed stories that mirror their own family lives. Of course, there are always plenty of animal stories to share. The Wiers are pet people. But we are not the kind of pet people who just have too many dogs; we have too many everything: a llama, horses, dogs, cats, a wolf, a bird, ferrets, guinea pigs, and one very grumpy pig. From this list, you might surmise that we live on a farm. We do not, much to the chagrin of some of our neighbors. We live in a country neighborhood with an unfenced yard where I am sure many have labeled us *that family.*

We try hard to keep our animals from being nuisances and have had moderate success: There was the Christmas the two stray dogs who adopted us stole our neighbor's UPS packages and ripped them open on our front lawn, or the time they brought home another neighbor's seven-foot inflatable Santa. But on the whole, most of our neighbors enjoy our menagerie, using us as a private petting zoo.

By far, the favorite Wier pet has been our sweet Great Pyrenees dog, Frodo. He was a gentle giant who not only protected the perimeter of our property but also socialized with all the walkers and joggers—often tagging along with them.

Just a few months before our oldest son's wedding, and during the busiest time of our lives, our beloved Frodo went to sleep at his guard post in the yard and did not wake up. Even though we had the comfort of knowing he lived a good long life and slipped away peacefully, we were heartbroken. That week I shared our loss in my column. A few weeks later, I received mail from a woman who lives two hundred miles away but whose parents live in our neighborhood.

Upon reading about Frodo's death, the parents saved the column for her to read since she was apparently well acquainted with our big dog. This stranger wrote, "Whenever we are in Nacogdoches visiting my parents, my husband and I walk the neighborhood in the evenings. We often saw your dog, whose name I never knew until your recent column. Over the years, he would occasionally join us for a bit. I never knew if he was kindly escorting us *away* from his property or if he was merely joining a friendly face for a bit. At any rate, every time he joined us, I considered it a true gift from God. I really adored that dog. . . . I know that all of you and I are not the only ones who loved him dearly. No one who met him could keep from loving him. A gift from God he truly was. My heart is with you."

While her letter was touching, it was even more convicting. My dearly departed dog had more of an impact on this woman's life than I did. My dog was acquainted with my neighbors' adult children, none of whom I knew. For years these strangers walked past my house, and the only one to greet them was Frodo.

The reality made me sad, especially because it wasn't always that way.

When we first moved to the neighborhood, I was determined to build relationships. With the help of a friend who lived a couple doors down, we had a strategy for getting to know our neighbors: We gathered family information and put out a community directory, we hosted a weekly neighborhood Bible study for women, and we organized a local ice-cream social. We believed God located us at our addresses so we could build impactful friendships—and we did.

Then life crept in and things got busy. As our kids grew older, their activities took more of my time. Soon it wasn't just my neighborhood friends I neglected; I had little time for the friendships I'd formed through years in our faith community. I stopped connecting with people who used to come to dinner, or those whom I had built trust with through years of prayer and concern for one another. As a couple, my husband and I also became too busy to cultivate the relationships with other couples with whom we used to spend quality time. Our new circle of "friends" consisted of our kids and their friends who hung out at our house. We still went to church. We were friendly to people at work. I still attended Bible study. I just didn't initiate one-on-ones with any of my friends during that busy time. I didn't deliberately disconnect; it just happened as I stopped intentionally connecting. Then the letter arrived revealing my dog's unlikely friendship, causing me to reflect on just how few of my relationships were active. Though I knew plenty of people, I was no longer sharing my life with them.

Coinciding with this revelation was my son's upcoming wedding, which brought into scope the consequences of my withdrawal from meaningful relationships. It was time to make the guest lists for the showers and celebration events. With a pen poised over the paper, a voice in my head that I know all too well began to taunt me. *No one wants to come to your events. You don't have friends. You didn't have time for them and now they won't have time for you.*

I hate that voice. It has been my companion most of my life, always there to persuade me that I am an outsider who doesn't belong—and it has had plenty of opportunities to speak up.

The Voice We Hear

As I was growing up, my family relocated about every two years. Since the age of five, I was the perpetual "new girl." Yet ever the optimist, I started each school year with the hope that I would finally find a BFF. A Best Friend Forever was the pinnacle of friendship success. To find that one person in the whole world who would pick me over everyone else, and with whom I could share my deepest thoughts and feelings, was what I wanted more than anything. The desire for that ideal BFF is one almost every little girl shares. It is also an elusive quest many grown women pursue, much to our peril. My own futile search for such a creature has been long and exhaustive, beginning with my early and frequent relocations.

At the start of every school year, with hopes that I would find "her," the search began anew. It took exactly one day in the lunchroom of a new school to realize "she" was taken. Everyone already had a soul sister. Pairs and groups of girls huddled together over bologna sandwiches, sharing their desserts and their secrets while I watched jealously from the new-kids' table. Breaking into a circle of friends was nearly insurmountable. Even at that young age, girls are protective over their friendship territory.

I remember what it felt like to be outside the circle then, but I have experienced it as grown-up Kim too. Little and big, I have felt the ache of longing to be included and the feelings of unworthiness that come with rejection. And the voice I heard then is the same voice I sometimes hear now: *If I were cuter, taller, smarter, funnier . . . if I were enough, I would have more friends.*

Maybe you've heard that voice too. Maybe it is an echo from the past or a new voice of insecurity that is holding you back. Let me say this, my sister—that voice is a liar. You are great friend material. God has created you as a unique reflection of himself as His personal gift to this world. Warts and all, you are His purposeful and pleasing masterpiece. His voice has once and for all declared the truth: "You are fearfully and wonderfully made." *That* is the voice to listen to. As we move forward together, we will learn to silence the other.

As a young girl, I listened to the lies in my head. The negative barbs coming from my insecurities rang loud and clear, so instead of trying to break into the fortress of established groups, I joined the other outsiders. In every school lunchroom, there seems to be a table inhabited by that random collection of kids who, for whatever reason, are not part of a group. These were always my people in the first few months of relocation. Sometimes I would make a real connection with someone in that group who would grow to be an actual friend. Often, we were all just placeholders for one another until an authentic relationship blossomed out of a contact on the playground or in reading group. The process was stressful and lonely until at long last genuine friendships began to grow. I wouldn't realize until much later that I learned valuable lessons from my repeated tenure at the outsiders' table.

You are great friend material. God has created you as a unique reflection of himself as His personal gift to this world.

My first taste of popularity came in high school as a result of our final relocation to a tiny town in central Texas. With only fifty-nine students in the graduating class, being the new kid had advantages. I was a novelty. Instead of being overlooked and ignored, I was sought out and included. For the first time, I had plenty of people to have lunch with and never lacked for a gal-pal with whom I could share secrets. It was everything I ever thought would make me happy.

I liked being liked. I was so elated to have friends that I tried to become all things to all people for fear of losing even one. With the friend who liked to gossip, I joined her with enthusiasm even while it made me uncomfortable. With my friend who never talked about anybody, I feigned ignorance of all social drama. I can't say I was authentic in any of my relationships. I was what I thought I had to be to keep friends. Even then the voice spoke: *If they knew the real you, they wouldn't want to be your friend*.

All these experiences have shaped not only the person I am now but also how I approached friendship for many years. Looking back has provided invaluable insights into many friend mistakes, and also given me a chance to unlearn bad friending habits.

The Risk We Take

For many women, what we struggled with as little girls was just a foretaste of what we encounter as grown-up girls. We want to be part of the group. We will respond to acceptance even when it comes in unhealthy ways. Our happiness is based on how much our peers like us. We believe about ourselves what others think is true. We reflect how others want to see us regardless of how we see ourselves. Avoiding loneliness can present compromise as a possible option. Just because we are all grown up doesn't mean we automatically know how to "friend" someone. In fact, unless we unlearn destructive and ineffective habits from the past, growing healthy, satisfying friendships in the future will remain difficult and frustrating.

In my experience, it takes just as much skill learning to enter into healthy friendships as it takes learning to be good at any vocation we pursue. Every passing year and every relationship, failed or fabulous, has taught me valuable lessons in the art of friending—even to the most recent lesson I learned from my dog.

Long removed from the lunchroom, the voice was again mocking me, this time because my dog was more popular than I. And so I sat staring at the list I had made for the first wedding shower, uncertain if anyone would come. In fact, I was sure they would not. Why should they? It's not as though I'd been a good friend to them in recent years.

I confessed my fears to one of the few friends who was active in my life and who was hosting the shower for my soon-to-be daughter.

"Susan, I don't think this shower is a good idea after all," I told her, echoing what the voice was whispering in my head. "I don't think anyone will come. I don't have many friends anymore."

> Just because we are all grown up doesn't mean we automatically know how to "friend" someone.

Susan assured me I was being ridiculous, reminding me I had lived in the same community for thirty years and attended the same church for twenty-five of those. "You have lots of friends, and they will all want to come," she said confidently. I wasn't so sure, but I gave her the list anyway. I desperately wanted these women to come meet our son's fiancée so she would feel loved and welcomed into his world.

Walking into my friend's beautiful home the day of the shower reminded me of walking into the lunchroom all those years ago. I felt I didn't belong. I prepared myself for the inevitable; but in fact, a room full of uninterested women was not waiting to greet us as I had expected. Instead, a room full of old friends enthusiastically stood ready to share our joy.

Even now, the memory of it brings me to tears. I had not been a real friend to any of them for at least two or three years, yet each chose to be a friend to me. That moment was the fruit born out of much previous life-sharing that, while paused, was renewed that day. It was renewed because I was willing to muster the little courage I had and risk asking for their friendship, and they were willing to step up and be a friend when I hadn't earned it. Freely given and freely received—a glorious aspect of life-sharing friendship. Another valuable lesson!

True or False?

Over the years I have made mistakes in pursuing friendships. One of the first was falsely believing that only a friend could meet my deepest needs, so I sought the elusive BFF. But I have made other blunders based on equally mistaken beliefs. Perhaps you have as well. Let's play a quick game of true-or-false. If we are going to pursue healthy, lasting friendships, we need to make sure we are aiming at the right mark. Which of these statements about friendships are true?

- All friendships are created equal.
- Quantity of time together equals quality of friendship.
- Friendship is worth compromising my values.
- True friends never leave you.
- A true friend will never let you down.
- Real friendships are born, not made.
- Being social is the same as being friends.
- True friendships are effortless.

If you said none are true, you are right. Yet these are fallacies we women embrace, and they lead to disappointing relationships. If you believe a true friend will never let you down, it won't be long before you doubt your friends who will invariably let you down. Not even the most reliable friend is perfect. However, if you expect that even your closest relationships will have some hurts and disappointments, you will be in a far better position to weather those rough patches than if you never expected they could occur. Look at the list again. Honestly consider if you have believed any of these friendship falsehoods. Such misunderstandings are the culprits of many friendship disasters.

Thank goodness we can learn from those mistakes and even use what we learn as we move forward to create more beautiful relationships.

Consider the friendships you are creating to be a form of art. The more you practice, the greater your perspective, the better the outcome. Unlike a science or a formula, art requires creativity, perspective, confidence, and even a measure of risk-taking. Every attempt will be unique, and each has the potential to display something beautiful.

A few years back I went to my first group paint party. The local artist sketched a rough outline of the picture we were to paint on our canvas and then offered suggestions on color and technique to get us started. I confess I have no natural talent, but with those suggestions and some patience, I was amazed at what I was able to create. Certainly, the piece had some flaws, but the great thing about working in acrylic paint is that once a stroke is dry, I could paint over it to make it better. The art of friendship is much the same. We begin with some principles as an outline and some suggested techniques, then we practice and adjust until we have something beautiful and unique to enjoy.

God created us for that kind of connection with one another, and He will help us find it.

As a Bible teacher myself, it was no surprise to find that the Master Artist has much to teach on the subject, and I made myself His apprentice. As I have invested in this amazing art form over the years, I have discovered my own talent at creating and keeping friendships. Stroke by stroke, I have learned from His hand the techniques of friendship. I have applied them in my own relationships and have seen those friendships take on new dimensions and life. As a women's ministry leader, I have been able to mentor women of all generations to do the same. Making meaningful connections is one of the most powerful ways to enrich our lives, and I have seen countless women transform their relationships with a few artful strokes.

Regardless of your previous experiences, you too can create the kind of friendships that add joy to the good times and comfort in the difficult ones. Even if you feel you have never been successful in building soul-sister relationships, I promise it is possible. God created us for that kind of connection with one another, and He will help us find it. All you need is courage and consistent effort. If you are willing to bring those two things to the table, then you are closer than you think to meeting one of the deepest needs of your soul—authentic life-sharing friendships.

2

Knowing Up from Down

Once, I ran out of gas twice in the same day—in the same car. First, I stalled out in a stranger's driveway while running the carpool. Being stuck on a hot day in a car full of stinky junior high boys is not something I recommend. Fortunately, the homeowner had a full gas can he eagerly shared to facilitate the expeditious departure of our van of rowdy teens from his drive. That scant gallon got me through my whole drop-off route, to the grocery store, and even to my daughter's soccer match. Rushing from place to place, I made a mental note to fuel up before I headed down the highway to the radio station where I host a live radio talk show.

I was about five miles outside of town when I ran out of gas for the second time in two hours. (Mental note number two: *Mental notes are not as good as sticky notes.*) In dire straits, I grabbed my cell phone and dialed my husband, but my battery was low and the phone died before the call connected. I finally got through long enough to yell, "Out of gas, near the river bridge, hurry!"

My husband eventually came to the rescue and I barely made it in time for the opening music of my radio show. If only I had paid attention to the low-fuel warning light on the dash.

The empty loneliness we feel without friends is a calling of our soul to satisfy a divinely inspired yearning. That kind of loneliness is like the low-fuel warning gauge on our cars. If we ignore it, we will find ourselves running on empty, often at critical times.

Our desire for friends is not just a superficial craving to have someone to go to the movies with or to vent to about the latest outrage our insensitive boss committed. Our longing for friends is actually a divine metaphor that God designed to prepare us for a much greater spiritual reality. Simply put, you and I long for friends because God put a craving for friendship in our DNA. We were divinely created to enjoy friends, so it's no wonder we aren't content without them.

God intends for friendship with one another to fuel something important in us.

God intends for friendship with one another to fuel something important in us. To deny, dismiss, or ignore this God-created longing comes with its own kind of spiritual consequence. Aloneness makes us vulnerable to discouragement, temptations, hopelessness, and even spiritual attacks. Without relationships to help cover our backs, sound the alarms, encourage, strengthen, and speak truth into our lives, we are more vulnerable than we were meant to be.

Shadowy Truths

One of the most famous gal-pal relationships in history comes from the Bible. Naomi had lost everything. Her husband uprooted her from her home and took her to live in a foreign country, where he died. Then her beloved sons died. She had no means to support herself, and sorrow upon sorrow left this woman of faith stranded in bitterness. She could not see proof of what she once believed—that God cared for her. Had it not been for the friendship of another woman, Naomi might have forsaken the hope and the future that God intended. Ruth came alongside Naomi and gave her the strength to keep moving forward. How did she do that? By moving forward *with* her. What once was a legal bond of mother-in-law and daughter-in-law grew into a friendship that helped Naomi resist discouragement, fear, and temptation. Without this beautiful friend walking the tough journey with her, Naomi's redeemed story might well have been very different from that recorded in the book of Ruth.

Friends are the fuel that keep us from being stranded in life. That is reason enough for us to take seriously our inner desire for friendships and take action. Finding ways to satisfy the God-given hunger for meaningful connections means developing a realistic picture of what adult friendship is supposed to look like.

But make no mistake, the plan for friendship is His plan—and like all things that originate with Him, it is far from trivial.

The full scope of God's blessings through friendship will not be fulfilled in the BFF goal of childhood that we so often still pine to achieve. God's life-sharing plan is so much broader and so much more satisfying. But make no mistake, the plan for friendship is His plan—and like all things that originate with Him, it is far from trivial. It not only meets the monumental practical needs of support and companionship, friendship also fills a unique spiritual tank we may or may not be aware exists in you and me.

To fully grasp the significance of this God-planned friendship need, we have to learn to think upside down. What I mean is we have to understand one of the great truths that sheds light on everything we experience as humans. Here is the truth: *What already exists "up" in the realm of heaven gives reality to what is "down" in the realm of earth.*

We often think that what we experience on earth might at some point be duplicated in heaven, but it is actually the other way around. Things that exist here are in actuality a reflection of a truer, greater reality that already exists in heaven. Heaven is the substance and earth is the shadow, not the other way around. This truth touches everything. Here are just a few ways Scripture describes this upside-down-ness.

- God provides bread for life because true Bread comes down from heaven to give life. (John 6:30–33)
- We gain insight from the horticultural realities of the vine because a Heavenly Vine sustains life. (John 15:1–2)
- On earth, a high priest was a shadow of the High Priest who sits at the right hand of God. (Hebrews 8:1)
- On earth, a tabernacle was patterned after heaven's true tabernacle. (Hebrews 8:2)
- On earth a law was given, but it is a shadow, not the reality itself. (Hebrews 10:1)

God uses earthly illustrations to reveal heavenly realities. We can find examples, which go on and on, in creation, in institutions, and in relationships. We mimic this kind of "teaching" all the time when we instruct our kids on concepts that are too complex for their state of maturity. We teach them to say I'm sorry as a small reflection of real repentance. We expect them to follow the rules at home as a shadow of keeping the laws of our country. We institute the act of earning an allowance to illustrate the greater reality that work has value.

Using examples, patterns, or shadows helps parents teach about complex concepts and realities. In a similar way, God teaches us about things that, right now, are beyond our full understanding. As Paul wrote,

> Now we see things imperfectly, like puzzling reflections in a mirror, but then we will see everything with perfect clarity. All that I know now is partial and incomplete, but then I will know everything completely, just as God now knows me completely. (1 Corinthians 13:12 NLT)

Without an understanding of this concept, we can get many things turned around. For instance, without this understanding, we could falsely believe that God as a Father patterned himself after earthly fathers, not the other way around. God does not call himself our Father because He is striving to relate himself to something in our reality. He never said, "How can I explain the loving caretaking role that I am able to fulfill in the lives of people? Oh, look. They have earthly fathers who take care of them. They understand the idea of children depending on their fathers and being loved unconditionally. I will point that out to them so they can understand my role. I will tell them I am like a father to them."

Patterning himself after our version of fatherhood would make Him a poor Father indeed. Rather, think upside down. God in eternity, outside of time, is Father, was Father, and always will be Father. He is the substance of all that is unconditional, benevolent, and protective. When, in time and space, He applied His imaginative force to the creation of the world, He instituted the relational function of fatherhood among humanity to explicitly serve as a shadow down here of the reality that already exists in heaven. Through that shadow we are able to understand, in part, an essential aspect of His nature: He is Father. What an incredible significance that adds to an earthly father's role. And what a responsibility fathers carry, knowing their role should reflect an aspect of God's character. That is just one example of God revealing heavenly realities using earthly types. In *Heaven*, Randy Alcorn described it this way:

> Often our thinking is backwards. Why do we imagine that God patterns Heaven's holy city after an earthly city, as if Heaven knows nothing of community and culture and has to get its ideas from us? Isn't it more likely that earthly realities, including cities, are derived from heavenly counterparts? We tend to start with Earth and reason up toward Heaven, when instead we should start with Heaven and reason down toward Earth.[1]

All things—visible and invisible, tangible and relational—were created through Him and for Him for the purpose of allowing spiritual realities to be "clearly seen, being understood from what has been made, so that people are without excuse" (Romans 1:20). Before the foundation of the world, God initiated fatherhood, marriage, family, friendship, community, governments, and other aspects of life that are essential to our humanness. These ideas predate the creation of the earth and mankind. They are eternal spiritual realities that have their origin in the dwelling place of God—that place we call heaven.

Grasping this concept and applying its significance is *upside-down thinking* that challenges our often earthbound, me-centric viewpoint and opens our minds to far greater realities. On the surface, we have come to know friendship for the practical function it serves. We can't buy friends, but we can go shopping with them. We can call one up if we are in a pinch for a baby-sitter. When we've got man problems, we cry on a friend's shoulder. When we are lonely, we speed-dial a friend who can keep us out of the gloomy abyss of self-pity. They help, encourage, warn, guide, and warm us.

Yet for all it offers, for most of us, friendship isn't a necessity like fuel in a car; we see it more as an optional luxury, like a car's navigator. We don't need one of those gadgets, but it sure makes the journey go smoother. That, in a nutshell, is the twenty-first-century synopsis of friendship: Friends are desirable but not essential. If, however, friends are merely an option, why are our lives so enriched when we have them and so diminished when we don't? It is because friendship is another of God's great object lessons intentionally written into the human story to illustrate for us in living color a great, grand, eternal truth: God is a Friend. Friendship isn't optional; it is essential.

Jesus, by no mere incidental comparison, calls us His friends:

> My command is this: Love each other as I have loved you. Greater love has no one than this: to lay down one's life for one's friends. You are my friends if you do what I command. I no longer call you servants, because a servant does not know his master's business.

Instead, I have called you friends, for everything that I learned from my Father I have made known to you. You did not choose me, but I chose you. (John 15:12–16)

One of the great overlooked doctrines of the Bible is God's friendship. Next to words like *justification* or *redemption* it sounds light, but nothing could be further from the truth. Friendship with God is the culmination, the climax, of many other doctrines. It is the ultimate luxury relationship with God we didn't think we could afford, only to discover it was bought and paid for with the blood of Christ.

One of the great overlooked doctrines of the Bible is God's friendship.

If you think something so wonderful is just too great to imagine, you would be right. It is beyond our human conception to fully understand all the implications of what it means to be a friend of God. But we can experience a shadow of that reality as we come into relationship with one another. Do you see the immense significance of experiencing friendships? It is through God's intentional gift of earthly friends that we get a glimpse of what He is offering us, consequently sparking a greater desire for His friendship. It's like licking the cake batter off the spoon. That is a treat in itself, but it also makes us even more excited about the promise of the cake to come.

Friendship is not optional. We are meant to *have* friends who reflect His kind of friendship, and we are meant to *be* friends so others can taste of God's kind of friendship. Having and being a friend carries great significance and responsibility in the same way as being a father or entering into marriage. All of these relationships show to the world something about the nature and character of God, and open windows for us to better understand great unseen heavenly realities. Friendship is a high calling indeed!

3

Friends Not Fads

Back in the day, *friend* was a word reserved to identify a person so valuable and so precious that it was preceded by the possessive pronoun *my*. *My friend* was someone who cared about me, who sacrificed for me, wept with me, and rejoiced with me. *My friend* was always a person who knew my weaknesses and still called me friend. *My friend* was someone who knew I peed in my pants at Walmart and kept my secret. *My friend* was someone I could call four times a day because my baby did the cutest thing—and each time *my friend* sounded genuinely happy to hear from me again. *My friend* was a person with whom I felt safe to share my insecurities and admit my fears.

Those are some of the things *friend* used to mean. Individual friends were so important that even in the midst of crazy busy lives, friendship found a way. I could bandage a scraped knee with one hand and hold the portable phone in the other just to ensure I stayed connected with an equally busy friend. I could settle an argument among my children with a snap of my finger and the stink eye while not missing a word of my friend's latest dilemma. Food preparation, discipline, kitchen disasters, and dogfights could swirl around, but the conversations carried on because there was a time when building relationships and sharing life was a priority.

One afternoon, a friend phoned to express concerns about her grandmother's illness, and her children interrupted.

"Mom, Duke won't walk with us," I heard through the receiver. The kids had been walking their cat on a harness when he lay down and refused to go. "We dragged him for a little while, but he still won't get up," they said.

Alarm rose in my friend's voice. "Quick, get me the scissors! The harness is choking him!"

The cat was unconscious and the scene sounded chaotic.

"Mom, why is Duke's tongue hanging out?"

"Why won't he stand up?"

"Mom, I can't find the scissors."

Still, it didn't occur to either of us to hang up. We were sharing the experience. As she hunted for scissors, I prayed for Duke. We were in it together. Finally, the cat was cut free and revived, and we went on talking about her grandmother. Duke, by the way, was fine.

That was then.

Now we are in the Facebook era, and *friend* has become a fad. They no longer come by the precious and personal handful; they come by the hundreds. They are not *my* friend, but *a* friend. As in, "How do you know Beth?" "Oh, she's *a* Facebook friend." On the surface, more sounds better. We can have more friends, instant access, low commitment, and best of all, be me-centered in a socially acceptable way. Seriously, who wouldn't want in on that kind of friendship? So far, more than a billion people have signed on to various social media platforms.

Even people who have actual friends get sucked into the virtual friend vortex. I did. Between raising a family, working, and doing ministry, I felt I was too busy to cultivate friendships. And along came Facebook. The virtual forum gave me a sense that I was putting that missing piece of the puzzle back into my life in a quick and easy way. Insta-friends were just the kind of relationships I had the time and energy to pursue. I connected with high school friends I hadn't thought about in decades. I suddenly knew what exciting things were happening to people I went to church with but never talked to. I would have never known my third cousin twice removed liked to go geocaching if it weren't for his constant location updates. And who knew my neighbor was obsessed with cat photos? I was really connecting.

As a social media newbie, I had no idea how posts were supposed to work, so mine were awkward. "KIM WIER is putting up Christmas decorations." "KIM WIER is procrastinating on a work project." I talked about myself in the third person until even I was bored. No surprise my updates solicited not one response. The few "friends" I had at the time chose to ignore my less-than-fascinating contributions. Now I felt rejected in a whole new way. I was no longer just disconnected from real friends, but even my virtual ones were disinterested in me. The urge to be "liked" by people online was compelling. I started thinking of ways my status updates could be entertaining, thought provoking, or inspiring. I posted stories about our pet llama. I made metaphors out of the cleansing nature of rain. I recommended books and shared charming anecdotes about my kids. I marvel at the depth of gratification I felt when any of my posts elicited a like, a comment, or—the holy grail—a share! Without realizing it, I was getting from these online friends what I used to get from real ones, namely acceptance and affirmation, however shallow and fleeting.

Though I never intended for these online exchanges to take the place of actual friendships, in many ways, they did. The interactions gave me the illusion that I was cultivating actual relationships. But of the 561 people who willingly called themselves a friend on Facebook, none were participating in my life any more than I was in theirs. None knew the agony I endured when my children were teetering on the edge, or the fear that threatened to consume me when life seemed out of control. They didn't know how hard it was for me to give my dad hope in his struggle with cancer. How could they? Those were not the kinds of things shared with the masses.

And that is what the social media community really is to most of us—a mass of people who know just a little about one another. In this format, we may garner some fans, but such one-dimensional relationships can never replace friends, no matter how many we accumulate. If we are not also cultivating those relationships offline, the fad falls far short of what authentic friendship offers.

> Anyplace you craft your image for social acceptance instead of authentic sharing will, at best, result in fans.

Social media is not the only place you can replace friends with fans. Maybe you did not get pulled online socially, but your approach in other groups has been to present a public persona meant to impress fans rather than cultivate friends. You can do this in church groups, at work, and in social settings. Anytime you craft your image for social acceptance instead of authentic sharing, it will, at best, result in fans. Having a big fan base can conceal the fact that you are running on fumes, but sooner or later the emptiness of those relationships becomes painfully clear.

Cost of Loneliness

We may be low on friends for other reasons. Too many commitments, season of life, a move, family obligations, or career building can all contribute to a lack of real friends. Maybe you have been hurt in a past friendship and have intentionally taken yourself off the friend market. Or a voice in your head tells you that you don't deserve friends or that you are not friend material.

You can even be so socially active that you have no time to grow deep friendships.

As a women's ministry speaker and a local women's ministry director, I have a unique vantage point on this reality. I interact with and get feedback from a wide cross section of women from all walks and seasons of life. From women who are financially secure to women who work multiple jobs; women who are married, single, divorced, and widowed; single moms, overwhelmed moms, frustrated moms, women who desperately want to be moms; women in the workforce and women on the home front; conservative women, liberal women, opinionated women, and quiet women. I have heard from them all, and I have worked to connect with them all.

In trying to reach such a diverse group, my job would seem almost impossible. It might be, except for one thing: They are all women. And that means they are all created by God to respond to and crave relationship—just as you and I do.

In our hyper-connected world, isolation is epidemic. All our connectivity has not alleviated our sense of aloneness; it has deepened it. We are connected to more people in more ways than ever before, yet we are lonelier and more disconnected. Communication in general has become impersonal with "get to the point" texts and emails taking the place of actual conversations, while social media takes the place of relationships. We are now a culture of a most ironic phenomenon: autonomous connection. We can connect from a distance without the inconvenience of participating in someone else's life.

> Think about what that means: Loneliness kills more people than obesity.

Many of us have developed these disconnected connections that come at a high cost—and not just relationally. According to research, loneliness is actually hazardous to your health. Studies show that the impact disconnecting from relationships has on the risk of death is comparable with such risk factors as drinking excess alcohol and smoking. In fact, isolation can be as bad for your overall health as smoking fifteen cigarettes a day. It even exceeds risk factors such as physical inactivity. Think about what that means: Loneliness kills more people than obesity. And still, we would rather admit we are overweight than admit we are lonely.

In the *Huffington Post*, Martha Edwards disclosed some paradigm-changing realities about the dangers of loneliness:

> Researchers are only now starting to pay attention to the importance of friendship and social networks in overall health. A 10-year Australian study found that older people with a large circle of friends were 22 percent less likely to die during the study period than those with fewer friends. . . . And last year, Harvard researchers reported that strong social ties could promote brain health as we age.
>
> Having meaningful relationships with friends . . . can help you live longer, and the more friends you have, the better. "There's been this notion that it's just those people who are 100% socially isolated who are at risk and that if you have one friend, you are OK. But this isn't the case," researcher Julianne Holt-Lunstad told *Forbes*. "People who have more, or more complex, social resources vs. people who have less, have higher rates of survival."[1]

The author concludes, "Exactly why friendship has such a big effect isn't entirely clear."[2]

I disagree with that conclusion. It seems very clear, especially when you realize that God designed us for friendship! God's Word is way ahead of research when it comes to understanding the dangers of being alone. How true is the proverb "Two are better than one, because they have a good return for their labor: If either of them falls down, one can help the other up. But pity anyone who falls and has no one to help them up" (Ecclesiastes 4:9–10).

John Milton once observed, "Loneliness was the first thing that God's eye named not good." It should be no surprise, then, that

4

Filling the Tank

When my friend Pam and I travel, we are determined to have a good time. Often, dazed bystanders are left in our wake, thankful to have survived the encounter. One brave man, however, was determined to get us into shape.

After a long three-hour layover, blessedly spent in the airline's President's Club, thanks to free passes Pam secured, it was time to hurry to our departure gate. We hated to leave that exclusive oasis reserved for the special people. We had a fabulous time, though it was clear we didn't fit in with all the suits encamped around us. They talked in hushed tones; we laughed out loud. They set out their portable offices; we had our pillows and fuzzy socks. They had briefcases; we had flotsam and jetsam. They were taking a break; we were having a party. I liked being special and was sad we had to leave.

But we lingered too long and now we were running to our gate, only to find when we got there they had changed the gate assignment. With all our debris hanging out of our bags, looking like refugees fleeing a war zone, we ran toward the opposite end of the terminal, making quite a scene—when miracle of miracles, an angel driving a shuttle cart offered us a ride. In seconds, we were flying through the airport, narrowly missing old ladies and babies in strollers, laughing and celebrating our good fortune. By the time we boarded the airplane, everyone else was already seated. Banging and bumping people as we scooted down the narrow aisle with overloaded bags in tow, we caught the attention of our soon-to-be seat buddy. Denial was in his eyes when he realized the two seats beside him were our destination.

"It's true," I told him apologetically. "We're your new flying friends. I'm so sorry."

After making a spectacle of trying to find space in the overhead bins, we finally settled in with our new best friend. He was a quiet, soft-spoken middle-aged man in a suit, who was intent on reading his book. Not wanting to be rude, I asked him a question or two, which he answered cordially. As the flight attendant announced what to do if the plane went down in a flaming fireball, I asked Mr. Man if he was returning home. He sternly put his finger to his lips and whispered, "I don't think we're supposed to talk during the presentation."

At first I thought he was kidding, but he was not. He really wanted me to give my full attention to learning how to use my seat as a flotation device as we flew over the desert southwest. People all around us were talking, but I was being shushed. Tickled by the absurdity of it, I had to muffle what became an uncontrollable laugh. The more I thought about it, the funnier it got. Tears spilled from my eyes as I turned to the window to hide my hilarious spasms from my seatmate, who was now reading the safety card. As the announcements concluded, Pam grabbed the *Sky Mall* magazine and engaged our Mr. Man in a diversion by asking him if he had ever ordered the jar of fake fireflies, guaranteed to provide hours of amazement for friends. No surprise, he had not. I laughed all the harder, no matter how much I tried to stop.

Pam understood and saved the day, and we had quite a good laugh about it afterward. Though Pam and I have our share of refreshing slapstick moments and fun girl trips, those alone won't go the distance in friendship. It is simply not enough. It is the wrong kind of fuel for the long haul. Thankfully, that is but one small part of our life-sharing relationship.

Learning from Our Model

My husband drives a humongous one-ton truck. It has six tires instead of four and can haul anything that can be hitched to it. I drive a small two-seat car. Whenever I need to take a road trip, we exchange vehicles. If the unthinkable happens on the highway, I want to be in the biggest tank possible. I have taken his truck more times than I can count, but every time I do, he reminds me what kind of fuel to get, as if I've never heard it before.

"Don't forget the truck takes diesel."

Never mind that the gasoline nozzle won't fit into the diesel fuel tank; he reminds me anyway. He knows that if for some crazy reason I managed to get gasoline into the diesel engine, it would ruin it. Gas and diesel are not interchangeable. The fuels consist of different ingredients, and if I want to get where I am going, I will make sure I put diesel in the engine because that is what it was created to run on.

If we want friendships that will fuel our body, mind, and soul in a way that helps us move forward, we need to fill up with the right kind of friendships.

If we want friendships that will fuel our body, mind, and soul in a way that helps us move forward, we need to fill up with the right kind of friendships. Pam is more than my slapstick friend. She is one of the women who has shown me what ingredients make up the kind of friendship God intended for us—the kind that models itself after Jesus.

Jesus, being the exact representation of the Father, is our model for the kind of friend we should seek as well as the kind of friend we should strive to be. Looking to Him gives us a starting point for moving forward in finding and growing friendships. We can see three aspects to how Jesus modeled friendship:

- *When* in history He demonstrated friendship offers insights into heavenly friendship.
- *How* He friended people shows how we should friend.
- *Who* He friended shows the type of person we should strive to friend.

When?

For our first insights, we can begin by looking at the time in history when Jesus entered into humanity as both God and man. God, who never does anything without purpose, uses even timing to intentionally amplify and clarify our understanding of His kind of friendship. Every age and every culture has defined friendship uniquely. While our modern concept of friend is more casual and optional, Jesus entered human history at a time in which friendship held the most sacred place in culture, society, and philosophy—the time when Greek and Roman philosophies reigned. Gail O'Day, dean and professor of New Testament and Preaching at Wake Forest School of Divinity, offered this explanation in her article "I Have Called You Friends":

> Friendship was an important topic in the Greek and Roman cultures in which the early church took shape and the New Testament documents were written. For Aristotle and classical philosophers who followed him, friendship was a key social relationship. In the democratic ideal of the Athenian polis, or city-state, friendship exemplified the mutual social obligation on which the polis depended. . . .
>
> For modern readers, Jesus' definition of love and friendship in John 15:13—to lay down one's life for one's friend—is completely

> unprecedented. . . . In the ancient world, however, Jesus' words articulated a well-known ideal for friendship, not a brand-new idea.[1]

Friendship in the cultural context to which Jesus was born had a universally accepted meaning with consequences not only for individuals but also for the well-being of the entire nation. The "friend" message Jesus would speak about and demonstrate resonated deeply in the priorities and value structure of the people of His day. First-century friendship was a far cry from the social-media demotion we have given it, whereby gaining and losing friends can be no more consequential than a mouse click. The Son of God could have entered the world at any historical point of His choosing. That He chose a time when the cultural concept of friendship best reflected the nature of His own divine Friend-ness was no accident. No culture before or since has regarded friendship with the intensity of that time. Yet again, God orchestrated the visible and invisible to make himself known, and then, in this case, became the living illustration himself.

All God's creations, including institutions, are more than one-dimensional metaphors. While they communicate by their form, they also have practical functions in the here and now. Marriage communicates to us that we are exclusively Christ's and will be eternally united with Him, but in function it does at least three things: It provides for God-designed procreation; it provides the foundation and structure of growing societies; and it is an ongoing illustration in the world of Christ's commitment to His bride—even if the world doesn't understand it. Friendship also has both a purposeful form and practical function that were best clarified in the historical context of Jesus' time.

The Greek word for "friend," *philos*, comes from the most common Greek word for "love," *phileo*. So in the language of the New Testament, the idea of friend was commonly understood to mean "one who loves." In form, friendship as embodied by Jesus delivers to us a powerful message about the nature and character of Jesus as the One who loves. As O'Day put it, friendship to Jesus was more than just words. Friendship wasn't just something He engaged in; it's who He was—and it's who He is. The Scripture record, she wrote, "illustrates how Jesus' entire life and death is an act of friendship."[2]

The Greeks and Romans held to this kind of ideal friendship philosophically, but Jesus did more than merely talk about laying down His life for His friends. Jesus inhabited the ancient ideal when He *did* lay down His life for His friends. Jesus' whole life is an incarnation of the ideal for friendship. The Greek and Roman model was a shadow of what Jesus was and is eternally, and in fullness. At the time, the two great philosophical dimensions of friendship were "giving one's life to one's friend," and equally essential, "sharing openly and honestly with one's friend."

How?

We have the great Gospel recounting of the literal laying down of His life by His own choosing as our model Friend. Jesus lived and died the truth of friendship that originates in heaven. That aspect is incredible and on many levels inconceivable in its scope and consequence. In fact, most of our Christian lives are spent in wonder of it. But in relation to friendship, let's not miss the other core truth shadowed in the common understanding of the day—*sharing honestly*. That was more than just a cultural requirement of the day. It was a reflection of a heavenly aspect of friendship. Jesus said we are His friends *because* He shared His knowledge of God honestly with us, and by that sharing transformed us into friends. He said,

> I no longer call you servants, because a servant does not know his master's business. Instead, I have called you friends, for everything that I learned from my Father I have made known to you. (John 15:15)

In an honesty that the philosophers of the time only conjectured about, Jesus delivered by sharing openly with His friends the mind and motives of God that He learned firsthand from His Father. His life as a friend fulfilled what philosophers could only theorize about.

Transparency isn't something at which most of us excel. I'm careful who I tell my kids' grades to, let alone my innermost thoughts and motives. Yet openness and transparency are the divine models of friendship. In fact, it is a prerequisite of Jesus' friends. According to Him, without that kind of honest sharing, we would still only be servants. His intimate disclosures signal that we are His friends. Are you astounded by that thought? The first time I wrestled with it my heart grew two sizes. I am a friend of God. God is my friend! Jesus has befriended me. I know the intimate thoughts of Creator God, my Savior. He chose me. Glorious!

No offense to you, but getting your approval no longer seems significant. I am a chosen friend of God, who shares His intimate confidence and for whom He has given His very life. The friend bar just got set very high, but not just for you; Jesus has also set the bar high for me. Both in word and deed, Jesus lived out the true model of friendship—the model that existed in heaven before we started practicing a shadow version with each other on earth. This is where the function of friendship is revealed. We don't just get to follow in Jesus' friendly footsteps; we are commanded to function as a friend according to His form.

> This is My commandment, that you love one another, just as I have loved you. Greater love has no one than this, that one lay down his life for his friends. You are My friends if you do what I command you. No longer do I call you slaves, for the slave does not know what his master is doing; but I have called you friends, for all things that I have heard from My Father I have made known to you. You did not choose Me but I chose you, and *appointed you* that you would go and bear fruit, and that your fruit would remain, so that whatever you ask of the Father in My name He may give to you. This I command you, *that you love one another*. (John 15:12–17 NASB, emphasis added)

Jesus became our friend freely by His own choice. He set the example as a friend that we should replicate it, albeit not perfectly; but perfection isn't the point. Obedience is. He told us to show the same kind of loving friendship so that fruit would be produced both in us and through us. That is our non-optional high calling to be a friend.

Facebook/Instagram/Twitter friendship does not qualify. Shallow, self-serving friendship does not qualify. Reserved, no-risk friendship does not qualify. The call is much greater, but don't despair. Calling us into His kind of friendship is like throwing Brer Rabbit into the briar patch. It might look scary, but the most wonderful adventure awaits because we were created for the briar patch. Our souls will find a new kind of fulfillment they have been craving as we embrace this life-sharing kind of friendship. At long last we will find friend satisfaction as we allow the Friend who lives in us to live out His friendship to others through us—and as we welcome the attempts of others to do the same.

Life-sharing friendship is richer and deeper because it is sharing the life of Christ in me with others in the midst of the everydayness.

Life-sharing friendship is richer and deeper because it is sharing the life of Christ in me with others in the midst of the everydayness. As His friend, Jesus has so enriched my life that I am a more valuable friend than I would otherwise be. I have been entrusted with the secrets Jesus shares with His Father. I see and experience life in more than one dimension. I have a Best Friend who has modeled for me putting friends first, being loyal, and not holding grudges. He has demonstrated sacrifice, intimacy, transparency, confidentiality, service, forgiveness, laughter, and celebration in friendship. All of His deposits in my life are things I can draw on as I share them with other friends and let them share with me. That kind of life-sharing friendship is compelling and irresistible.

The challenge is to learn, sometimes through trial and error, how to draw on that divine model for our earthly friendships.

We've looked at the *when* and the *how* of that model. In the next chapter, we will focus on the *who* of Jesus' friendships to guide us in the pursuit of the people around us.

Every aspect of His friendship is instructive. The more we discover Jesus as the inventor and source of friendship, the more we will find implanted in us the ability to offer more to others and to receive more. Sister, it is time to fill up your friendship tank!

5

The Who's Who List

Several years back I became acquainted with a most remarkable woman. Mary McCleary was a university professor (now emeritus) and is a renowned American artist. Her specialty is mixed-media figurative collages. Her works have been displayed all over the country. Incredibly, she lives in our small community. I was thrilled to visit her studio. Though I had seen photographs of her work, I still didn't understand what "mixed media" meant. The pictures looked more like a combination of portrait and mosaic. I couldn't imagine how she had gotten the striking effect. I couldn't wait to see them in person. When I did, I was speechless. Her work truly must be experienced. She usually works on a framed surface ranging from six- to eight-feet wide and equally tall. These are large impact pieces. Yet here is the irony: These large portrait-style pictures are made up of hundreds of individual objects applied with precision to create a singular whole.

What first appears like a painting of something ordinary—say, a woman holding a birthday cake—is actually hundreds of disparate objects perfectly arranged to communicate one cohesive message.

Beads, buttons, marble, glass, sticks, plastic toys, paper, string, and other items too numerous to list are painstakingly applied one by one with intentionality of texture and color. When you stand close to the work you can see and identify each and every one. When you stand back, however, all the individual pieces meld together so perfectly in their placement that they give way to something else entirely—a woman with a cake, for instance.

In addition to the magnificence of this incredible technique, the collage is also fraught with symbolism to convey something far deeper than a mere image to admire. It must be experienced to truly appreciate the way she has made the whole greater than the sum of its parts.

Friendship is meant to be like Mary's masterpieces. The whole portrait of our friend-life is made up of a variety of different pieces. No two friendships in the picture are the same. Each has a unique color and texture and fits into a specific place in your life. Up close, it has a character and definition all its own. But when you step back and take in the scope of your entire friend-life, you see a completely different picture. All of our friendships, when seen as a whole, are a mosaic that is a faint but enlightening reflection of God's divine friendship. It takes a whole bunch of us to try to reflect a little of Him. And just like a stick is not a bead or a marble, neither is one friend the same as another. Yet each has its essential place in the big picture. As we begin to evaluate the state of our friendships, it is important to value the differences and embrace the concept that out of many will come the beautiful picture of friendship for which we long.

Making the List

The first step in growing an active and significant mosaic of life-sharing friends is to think about who is in your life now. Even if many of your relationships are not deep and significant now, that doesn't mean they won't be in the future. Remember Pam, sidekick in my airplane story? For several years she would not have been even a potential soul sister. God had other plans. Now she is not only one of my closest friends, she is a beloved ministry partner. God has woven our lives together in a way that when I'm cut, she bleeds. I never saw it coming. When I met her, she seemed like a hair-flipping sorority type that I would have nothing in common with. I couldn't have been more surprised at what developed over time. It turned out we both loved serving in women's ministry. We both became moms. We both loved working in kids' programs. And mostly, we both loved to study God's Word. Serving in the same church family, we were always going in the same directions. Time and circumstances turned two women who were complete opposites into two women who complement each other's strengths and weaknesses. We laugh now and say that together we make one complete person. Time, circumstance, and priorities changed our relationship.

It is key to understand and embrace this change dynamic. If I were to go back to the day I received the Frodo letter, my first inclination would be to say I didn't have many relationships that I could put on a list. Maybe you feel that way now. Your life circumstances may be such that you have more inactive relationships than you do active ones. That's okay. It's possible that the root of those friendships is still alive and waiting to be revived. Consider those people as being in your life right now for a reason. It's also possible that some former relationships truly have no revivable connection, either by choice or circumstances—maybe a friendship ended because of a conflict or betrayal, or maybe someone moved and you don't keep in touch on a recurring basis. But there are probably a variety of people you should put on your list of connections, even if those connections have grown stale or are only a seed.

As we begin to think about creating a list of relationships we currently have, let's consider how we could categorize them. In the life of Jesus, the first Friend, we see that He had a mosaic of all kinds of friendships. His friends came from different social strata, were male and female, had differing backgrounds and even different religions; some were very similar to Jesus and many were very different. There were also varying degrees of closeness among these diverse connections. While He shared His life with all of them, the sharing was not equal. That, however, did not make any relationship insignificant. So as you think about your current relationships, don't write anyone off simply because you don't have a deep connection with them. There is a place for them in your friend life. Having a broad friend portfolio is a greater aim than one BFF. The goal is to have many kinds of friends at varying levels of intimacy. Some friendships will help you grow. Some will be an investment you make to help them grow. And some will be those balanced rare jewels. You can be committed to all of them even though the relationships are not equal.

Some friendships will help you grow. Some will be an investment you make to help them grow. And some will be those balanced rare jewels.

So get out your favorite fancy journal and make a list. Or if you don't have one, roll off a piece of TP or use the back of a receipt. (And by the way, that would make you perfect friend material for me.) It doesn't have to be a fancy list, but taking time to evaluate the state of your relationships is essential to growing them.

Let's break it down using the groupings Jesus embraced. You may or may not have people in all of these categories. No worries. That's why we are doing this—to search for the opportunities to broaden our life-sharing friendships. To help illustrate this process, in addition to sharing examples from Jesus' life, let me share with you how my own friendships fall into this mosaic through a snapshot of one event in my life: my father's death.

It was during one summer when my dad, a joyful and vibrant guy, was diagnosed with an aggressive cancer. Although the doctors were clear that less than 40 percent survive even a year, we remained hopeful as he went through all the treatment protocols. Years of smoking, though, complicated his progress with respiratory issues. In the end, the cancer could not be stopped. Just forty-eight hours after we learned that the cancer had moved to an untreatable stage, Dad went into respiratory failure. He had felt great despite the prognosis, and we thought we would have months to say our good-byes. Instead, he was suddenly on a respirator, only semiconscious and declining quickly. We had hours, not months. It was in those last hours and in the days that followed that our kaleidoscope of friends swirled around us in a most beautiful display of love and care.

More than ever, I came to appreciate the variety of friendships that make up my life. Yes, the kindred spirits were there, but so were many other kinds of friends, and each practiced Jesus' kind of "loving one another" in their own way at their own level of intimacy. One BFF could never have covered us in the kind of love the diverse types of life-sharers showed, meeting us in our every need. While one was ever-present at my side, others showed Christ's love in other ways. Some prayed. Some sat by my dad's bedside. Some cried with us in the waiting room. Those who were closest to me were my needed emotional support. Those not so close found a place in meeting more practical needs. Even those I would consider more casual friends as part of our church family lent their support by being present at the funeral. Individually, each played a part. Altogether, God showed himself a friend to me through those who gave their friendship.

Which is better: the illusive unicorn known as the BFF, or the mosaic of valued people who share your life, each giving a little of themselves and receiving a little of you? You already know the answer. So let's look closely at who makes up the picture in your life. We will start with those who are closest and work our way out.

Inner-Circle Friends

This is a small number of people, perhaps two to five, with whom you share the greatest depths of yourself, and they share theirs with you. Anne of Green Gables called these "bosom friends" and "kindred spirits." In Jesus' life, John, Peter, and James were in His inner circle. He shared more intimate moments with them than with anyone else.

When Dad was taken to the hospital, we entered crisis mode. His blood pressure dropped and he lost consciousness. The medical team rushed him into heart surgery, concerned a blockage was causing the major problems. It was the middle of the night, and my sister and I had to make all the decisions. It was excruciating to watch him in such a helpless state. Dad was a vibrant man, in many ways bigger than life. He stood 6 feet 4 inches, with salt-and-pepper hair, and had a charming and jovial manner that made others gravitate toward him. Even greater was his heart. This was especially precious to us because it had not always been that way.

Raised by an abusive father, Dad struggled to find his own value, to the point that he sabotaged all of his relationships. My parents divorced when I was very young, so we saw Daddy only on holidays and a couple of weeks in the summers. Though we knew he adored my sister and me, picking up the pieces of his personal life took most of his focus. He missed the best parts of being a father. It wasn't until we were grown with children of our own that a miracle took place that gave us the dad we never really had.

Broken and broke for the umpteenth time, my father finally bowed in repentance to his heavenly Father and accepted new life, and a new heart, through a personal relationship with Jesus Christ. He was fifty-five years old with no worldly assets, and for the first time in his life he had joy—and he had a plan. He wanted to experience being part of his family. So he packed his few belongings and joined us in Texas to start fresh. For twenty years, God gave my dad back all he had missed with my sister and me. He got to be an everyday grandpa to his five grandchildren. He was at every school event, sports game, birthday, and holiday. He was at their graduations and the first grandchild's wedding. It was a glorious thing to behold. And only a few of my close friends knew the fullness of this beautiful story of redemption. To everyone else, my dad was just Big John, the guy who loved God and loved people.

When he died, the true depth of my loss could be shared only with those who really understood. Of course, dear Pam was in the hospital waiting room before I even had a chance to call her. Like a true intimate, she didn't ask what I needed. She just held my hand. She knew when to laugh and when to cry, when to step up and handle something and when to fade into the background. She knew me and she knew my dad stories.

Another friend, Susan, poured her sorrow for me into service to my family, but again needed no instructions. Susan's great gift was prayer, prayed from the heart of a daughter who also had a dad residing in heaven. Many times we had talked about how special our daddy-daughter moments were to us. She had her weekly lunches with her father, and I had my Saturday morning coffee dates with my dad on the front porch of our home. Susan and I had also talked about those time-to-time frustrations adult kids feel with parents, so she knew I would have guilt over any annoyance I ever felt. She headed it off with gentle cautions not to let myself feel that way.

While Pam and I had been a duo for twenty years, Susan had been a sweet friend and confidant for only five. But time does not determine categories. Intimacy does. On a day-to-day basis, these are the girls in my inner circle—incredibly different, but equally treasured. I let them into the deep places of myself that are too small and intimate for a crowd.

Others fit this category even though we don't have the luxury of everydayness. My two college roommates, Becky and Gaye, have been constants in my life since I was eighteen years old. We have stayed close for thirty years, buoying each other in the tough times and soaring together in the joys. I stood by both of them as each buried her daddy, and they crossed miles to stand beside me when it was my turn. There is a trust and strength in our cord of three strands that is priceless beyond measure.

Finally, in this exclusive group is one of the shining lights of my life, Michelle. We were young married women together, had our babies together, grew up in the Lord together, and transitioned to empty nests together. We have long since lived in different towns, but through prayer and regular phone chats, we remain connected at the soul in the most intimate of friendships. She knows the things I don't even like to tell myself. I have no need to pretend with her—ever.

These five women encircled me every moment as I let go of my daddy, each carrying parts of my story no one else had. These are the women who make up my inner circle.

- Who are the people in your life you feel you can trust with the most authentic you?
- Who would you call if something wonderful or tragic happened because you know that person would understand how you were affected?
- Who would you call on in your time of greatest need without the worry that you would inconvenience them?
- Who would you drop anything for in their time of need?

Close Friends

Also a small group, these are people closest to you outside of your inner circle of friends. This is a group characterized by intimacy and a growing relationship of trust and loyalty. For Jesus, this group included the remaining nine disciples (yes, even Judas), Mary, Martha, and Lazarus. Jesus' group of close friends—not counting His intimate friends, Peter, James, and John—numbered twelve; ours will likely be fewer.

As soon as word got out that I was at the hospital with my dad, a few women jumped into action. Twelve hours into the crisis, I went into the ICU waiting room to find it had been taken over on our behalf. A couple of dear friends whose intimacy did not extend into the actual hospital room knew what else we would need: comfort food. They had catered the waiting room with snacks, coffee, sodas, candy, and barbecue. They did not wait to be asked how they could help. They knew us. They knew all of our kids and extended family would keep vigil with us, so they made sure our practical needs were met so we could keep our focus on Dad and one another. These sweet gals didn't just drop food off and go—they sat for hours to be nearby in the event a need arose. They kept the conversations going when they knew we needed a distraction. They prayed silently over every decision that came up over those forty-eight hours. And when the time came, that same spirit of hospitality and care moved from the hospital to our home. They made sure we had meals, and then handled providing a beautiful lunch after Dad's memorial.

I felt such comfort as I watched their sweet forms glide in and out of the room as we went about the business of good-bye. Their presence was a strength because these were all women who know the real me. We hang out for girls' nights. We help problem-solve in one another's lives. Some I've known for a long time, some not long at all. Each friendship started in a unique way with its own story and grew through shared experiences. These are sweet, growing, personal, bosom relationships. So of course, they would be at the heart of a crisis in my life, carrying any part of my burden to keep the load from crushing their close friend.

- Who besides your inner circle do you consistently find time for and seek out?
- Who consistently finds time for you?
- Who not in your most-trusted inner circle would you trust to share a confidence?
- Who do you enjoy spending large amounts of time with?
- Who trusts you to have their back?

Shared Friends

This is your social group that you have in common with others. These are people you consistently spend quality time with in some capacity, often because they know others in your circle. They are people you enjoy but in whom you do not place your unconditional trust or confidences, either by choice or because time limits your ability to invest in more than a few intimates. This is a group of probably five to fifteen people. For Jesus, this group included His mother, His brother, His family members, Nicodemus, Mary Magdalene, and the other women who followed His full ministry.

As our church's women's ministry leader, I have gotten to know many women I might not have crossed paths with otherwise. I regularly spend time with those on the leadership team through our common ministry commitment. Through that shared interest, I have the chance to make something of those relationships. As we have gone about our ministry focus, we have begun to share our lives with each other. When my dad was swept up into heaven, several of these women continued to grow their friendships with me by taking that opportunity to share my loss. They brought food, they sent cards, and even though they didn't know my dad, they came to the funeral and sat together in a silent display of solidarity. Shared relationships can move to close friendships and even, sometimes, to inner-circle friendships.

- Who are your shared friends?
- With whom do you often interact in a shared social group?
- With whom do you serve on a regular basis in a church setting or community setting?
- Do you have a work associate you engage with often?
- Who do you consistently run into at social functions through your shared connections?

Casual Friends

These are people you are acquainted with by name and familiar with through unintentional friend avenues, such as work, church, or associations, whose friendship would likely end if the link by which you are connected was broken. This could be a group of a few to over a hundred. For Jesus, this group included Peter's mother, individuals He met among the crowds, Simon the leper, Zacchaeus, and the unnamed disciples who followed after Him regularly.

When my daddy let go of the cords that tied him to this life, he was surrounded by family and intimate friends, both his and ours. Encircling his bed in the ICU, we thanked God in one spirit for the incredible man who was our dad, grandpa, and friend. We praised God for His faithful care and compassion in bringing the man we loved so much into His family as well as ours. Everyone in that circle knew my dad's life was a testament to the power of redemption. Then, just a moment after that final amen, my daddy breathed his last breath in our presence and his first breath in the presence of God. It was an incredible life experience we shared with those who stood on that painful, remarkable, holy ground with us. It is the kind of life-sharing experience that takes deep relationships deeper.

Though such things are too intimate to share at large, we could share other things, the less intimate places, at his memorial celebration with many people we consider casual friends. This included people we have gone to church with for many years. Some I have known longer than a few of my close friends, but again, duration does not dictate intimacy. Though I have known them longer, I do not know them better. I care about them and have had a level of relationship with them through our common faith community.

Other casual friends whom we shared more publicly came from my work circle. None of them would be on my short list for a Friday night dinner, yet we share life at a certain level on a regular or semi-regular basis with a genuine congeniality and care. If they moved churches or jobs, we would likely not continue our casual relationships without the regular interactions, but that doesn't mean I don't value each. They offered a comfort that they chose to voluntarily participate in this life event; one day, some of these relationships might grow to the next place of intimacy.

This casual friend list is most likely too large for you to make, but consider these insights in recognizing such relationships:

- These are people who receive a form of your friendship, thus some of your time and energy.
- Expectation about these friendships should be limited to their current scope.
- Potential deeper friendships may be lurking in this list, so take note.

Acquaintances

These are people we see intermittently. While we may be friendly, we have no active, ongoing friendship with them. For example, occasionally I see people at Walmart whom I know by name from past associations but now only see at Walmart. Though sharing a price rollback is thrilling, it is not the basis for even the most casual kind of friendship. It is an occasion for a friendly greeting. These people require no ongoing friend maintenance on our part.

Rivals

Some people call this group enemies, but I'm from the South. We don't have enemies; we have rivals. You know you have a rival when she talks about you and adds that all-too-condescending phrase *Bless her heart*. Others would call such a rival a frenemy, but I reject that title. It implies friendship on the surface and rivalry underneath. That kind of falseness is what Jesus called a wolf in sheep's clothes. Trust me on this one: We actually adopted a wolf, and I could dress him up like Little Bo Peep, but he would still act like a wolf. If we know who these women are, then we should call them what they are. There is no such thing as a hybrid friend. Take them off your friend list. Remember the characteristics of Jesus' model of friendship—truth and sacrifice. A frenemy offers neither.

This list should be short because if it is long, it is likely you may actually be the problem. So don't move past this list too quickly. Make sure you have not been the one burning bridges, behaving falsely, or causing offense. If God brings something to your mind, go and restore the relationship with some good old-fashioned humility. Friends are a valuable commodity not to be squandered. In addition, remember your calling—to be a friend in the form and fashion of Jesus himself.

Others

Finally, there are innumerable people yet unknown who are potential friends. Always be watchful as God brings new people into your life.

Your Project

Take time to work on your list so you have a visual of the scope of the varied relationships you already have. Don't get mired in trying to reach a number in each group. Just honestly place names in categories you feel best describe the kinds of relationships you currently have. After you're done, ruminate on this list. It is the starting place from where your friend life will grow. Take time to thank God for each person already in your life, and ask for wisdom as you begin the brave step of creating and keeping meaningful relationships.

6

Friend Yourself

There is one more person with immense friend potential we need to assess. This often-overlooked gal is the most important person in your strategy to developing lasting and meaningful friendships. How you feel about her will affect every current and potential relationship you enter into.

She is you.

Earlier I shared with you about the voice in my head. It is the voice of a little girl, insecure and scared. She makes me doubt. She picks on my appearance. She tells me I'm not really wanted. All of us have a self-doubting voice. Maybe yours sounds like your mother, a harsh sibling, a sixth-grade rival, a critic, or someone who has wounded you; or maybe it's the voice of a comparing and condemning culture that takes every opportunity to whisper that you don't measure up. The voices we hear are echoes of both our fears and our scars. They are born out of experiences or perceptions, and unchecked, grow into damaged destinies.

But you have to acknowledge one more thing about that voice in your head: The voice is yours. While it is informed by your emotions and your experiences, it is formed in your own mind. This

> The voices we hear are echoes of both our fears and our scars. They are born out of experiences or perceptions, and unchecked, grow into damaged destinies.

is actually good news. It means you have control. Perhaps you couldn't stop your mother from criticizing you, but you can stop your own inner impersonation of her from taking the stage in your mind every day.

Comedian Jim Gaffigan has made a career in stand-up by letting the audience into the voices in his head. As he tells stories of his day-to-day life, the narrative is interrupted every few thoughts as his high-pitched, distinctly feminine "inner voice" speaks out in a running commentary of critical diatribes, judging, criticizing, second-guessing, and berating. In a recent comedy special, upon receiving a rousing applause from the audience, Gaffigan and the voice spar.

Gaffigan: "Oh my gosh, you make me feel only twenty pounds overweight."
Inner Voice: "Oh, look at his beard. He's—"
Gaffigan: "He's got quite a beard."
Inner Voice: "He looks like an out-of-shape Civil War general."[1]

The criticism is funny. Very funny, in fact. But it is also too familiar. You see, his voice is born from his reality. When asked about the source of that comedy shtick, he admitted that the voice often impersonates his sister, who was an early influencer. But she isn't the only one. He confessed, "I think I have a lot of voices in my head, and I guess my inner critic is a female." Me too, Jim. Me too.[2]

If I were to let my inner voice speak out loud, she would be just as harsh, just as persistent, but not nearly as funny. In fact, she isn't funny at all. She is mean, just as I assume yours is. So unless we can find a way to harness that voice and make a living from it like Gaffigan, we must learn to muzzle it.

The Voice of Truth

Some have suggested that the inner voice of criticism can actually be a healthy motivating force, but let me tell you why that cannot be true. As a follower of Jesus, He has promised us that in our relationship with Him, there is no condemnation. He is Light and He is Truth, and when He takes up residence in our lives through His Spirit, He operates in light and truth.

> This is the message we have heard from him and declare to you: God is light; in him there is no darkness at all. If we claim to have fellowship with him and yet walk in the darkness, we lie and do not live out the truth. But if we walk in the light, as he is in the light, we have fellowship with one another, and the blood of Jesus, his Son, purifies us from all sin. (1 John 1:5–7)

Wow. That is a jam-packed passage for the girl looking for relationship advice. First, if you want to have fellowship with the Friend who takes first priority, you can't walk in darkness because in Him there is no darkness. Keeping company with the false accusations of your inner critic keeps you from walking in close fellowship with God. If, though, we walk in light, yielding to what is true and enlightened by Him, we not only walk with Him, "we have fellowship with one another." Bonus!

Self-condemnation, fear of judgment, voices of unworthiness, self-hatred, and self-doubt creep out of places of darkness. Unlike your conscience, which provides constructive guidance, you can recognize your inner critic by her deprecating tone and isolating effects. Even if that voice moves you to some kind of positive action, it comes at the cost of fear, self-intimidation, or self-worth.

God has never sought to bring us to growth and maturity with those methods. He is the Friend who draws us into His likeness with kindness, gentleness, and patience. Even when He brings conviction and discipline regarding our sin and weakness, He does it with compassion and grace. Why? Because He created a most remarkable person whom He values.

Is it possible that the isolation and frustration you may feel, and the difficulty you may have in finding intimate friendships, is rooted in your surrender to self-criticism?

Such inner oppression leaves us desperate for affirmation and acceptance. Yet we can never satisfy that need because the inward negative flow will always be greater than what our outward quest can provide. Far from drawing healthy relationships, the vacuum of self-worth is a catalyst for demanding more than others can give. Often, we are left finding consolation in other vacuous souls, creating dysfunctional relationships of desperation or no relationships at all.

If any of this resonates in your heart as the truth of your circumstance, you have a way out of the darkness. You can position yourself for the intimacy you long for with God and others "if [you] walk in the light, as he is in the light, [then you] have fellowship with one another."

Walk in the light of what is true about you. Come out of the darkness of self-criticism. You might guess that while the answer is simple, it is not easy. Your inner critic has been doing her shtick for a long time. She will only get off the stage when you stop being her audience. The problem is her act is so compelling. Turning a deaf ear will take diligence and help. We all need an assist now and then when we feel weak or particularly vulnerable. Maybe you have experienced this kind of help to overcome your weakness in regard to sweets, or maybe an addiction to screen time, or even taming your tongue. Having someone to help can make all the difference.

Truth or Consequences

A few years ago my friend Gaye and I decided to kill time at the nearby Galleria. This is no ordinary mall with loitering teens or mall walkers. It is a sophisticated shopping mecca filled with upscale stores catering to upscale shoppers, all staffed with solicitous sales consultants eager to offer expert assistance. After browsing for a couple of hours, we unwittingly stopped to admire a beautiful ensemble in a store window.

"Ladies," crooned a welcoming female voice from the doorway, "you must come in and look around. Today is our grand opening."

"Thanks, but we're just window shopping," I demurred, as she physically corralled us toward the doorway.

"We're serving the most wonderful hors d'oeuvres and champagne. We are so glad you're here." And before we knew it, we had been ambushed by a Galleria glamazon. Everywhere we looked we saw beautiful clothes and beautiful people.

"Your models are gorgeous," Gaye commented.

"Oh, those aren't models. Those ladies are the Who's Who of Dallas here for our opening."

That was all the small talk we were allowed. Glamazon Audrey appointed herself my personal shopper, held up a dress, and declared, "It's simply made for you."

I had to admit, it was fabulous. Seeing she had my attention, she escorted me to a luxuriously appointed dressing room (and put Gaye in another) and returned in a flash with strappy gold shoes to complete the ensemble. As I modeled my new look, sales experts surrounded me, pulling and tugging and deciding as a group I needed a smaller size, declaring me "petite." Oh, they were good! The problem was that this was not a shop that fit my budget.

Still, the fawning voices continued unabated. I was the queen, and flattery flowed liberally, as did the fashion selections. When I put on Audrey's next pick—a linen skirt, drape-neck top, and fitted jacket—I looked and felt like a million dollars, and my resolve began to crack. The voice telling me my life would not be complete without that suit started echoing in my own mind. I was in trouble.

After making sure the sales posse didn't spot me, I dashed across the hall to Gaye's dressing stall. In whispers, we raved at my fabulous outfit and the wonderful haute couture she was modeling. We took pictures knowing we might never look so good again and laughed about our predicament of being held captive by beautiful people. Then I confessed that I was starting to believe all their flattery and was tempted to break the bank on the clothes.

"No. We've got to get out of here," Gaye said. "You don't need those clothes and neither do I. We're already awesome. Maybe not as well-dressed—but awesome!"

Our strategy to get away with our money intact was to stick together, not let them divide us again, and to leave immediately. So after changing back into our own drab clothes, we left the dressing room arm in arm—and ran right into Audrey.

"Ladies, what shall we ring up today?" she said, corralling us again. "You have so many great options."

Gaye was polite but firm. "Yes, we do. In fact, we're going to dinner right now to think about it."

Girl, the self-critic in your head is not your friend.

With that, she gave my arm a little tug, and we walked out of that boutique and away from the voices that tried to reimagine us. Audrey and her colleagues had played the parts of trusted girlfriends, flattering and pretending, to influence my actions. But Gaye's intervention reminded me that "the righteous choose their friends carefully, but the way of the wicked leads them astray" (Proverbs 12:26).

Girl, the self-critic in your head is no more your friend than the glamazon was mine. That voice will lead you astray. There is a Voice, however, that will not. You have a righteous Guide who is your friend and who will not only speak truth to you, but who also will support you so you can act on that truth. He can help you not just resist that critical voice, but also change her message. Remember, she is you, and the key to changing what you say to yourself is learning what is true, believing what is true, and then dwelling on what is true.

It is time to befriend yourself with truth! It might take some time, but you are not fighting the lies alone. God says He is the "friend who sticks closer than a brother" or a sister (Proverbs 18:24). Through His Holy Spirit at work in you, He will shine truth and light into the dark places. Like the psalmist, we can proclaim,

> I waited patiently for the LORD; he inclined to me and heard my cry. He drew me up from the pit of destruction, out of the miry bog, and set my feet upon a rock, making my steps secure. He put a new song in my mouth, a song of praise to our God. Many will see and fear, and put their trust in the LORD. Blessed is the man who makes the LORD his trust, who does not turn to the proud, to those who go astray after a lie! (Psalm 40:1–4 ESV)

Pause to Ponder

Are you ready for God to put new, true words into the mouth of your inner voice? Then let's look at the truth and ask God to make it illumine your heart and mind. Pause and ponder each of these truths from God's Word. Think about the questions. Perhaps even get out a journal and write your thoughts. Have a conversation with your Friend about what lies you have believed and what truths He wants you to embrace. Don't be in a rush. You can move forward when you are ready.

> Whoever gets sense loves his own soul; he who keeps understanding will discover good. (Proverbs 19:8 ESV)

- Do you believe God wants you to love your own soul?
- In what ways does it make sense that you should love yourself?

> No one ever hated his own flesh, but nourishes and cherishes it, just as Christ does the church. (Ephesians 5:29 ESV)

- How does Christ cherish the church?
- In what ways is that a model for you to love your own flesh?

There is no fear in love, but perfect love casts out fear. For fear has to do with punishment, and whoever fears has not been perfected in love. (1 John 4:18 ESV)

- What fears speak loudly to you?
- How does God's perfect love for you address each fear?

Above all these put on love, which binds everything together in perfect harmony. (Colossians 3:14 ESV)

- What do you think is required for you to put on love in place of self-criticism?
- Where do you lack harmony with God?
- How could seeing yourself through His eyes bring harmony?

Anyone who does not love [even themselves] does not know God, because God is love. (1 John 4:8 ESV)

- How does this admonition elevate the importance of learning to love even yourself?
- In what ways can God teach you to love as He loves?

Let all you do be done in love. (1 Corinthians 16:14 ESV)

- How can self-critique be done in love?
- In what ways can you lovingly befriend yourself?

Since we are surrounded by so great a cloud of witnesses, let us also lay aside every weight, and sin which clings so closely, and let us run with endurance the race that is set before us. (Hebrews 12:1 ESV)

- What specific weights of self-criticism do you need to lay aside?

- How can focusing on running ahead keep your thoughts under control?

I . . . urge you to walk in a manner worthy of the calling to which you have been called, with all humility and gentleness, with patience, bearing with one another in love. (Ephesians 4:1–2 ESV)

- What manner of thinking is worthy of a child of God and a coheir with Christ?
- What should you confess as unworthy thinking?
- Will you ask God to help you understand your favored position as His child and His friend?

If anyone would come after me, let him deny himself and take up his cross and follow me. (Matthew 16:24 ESV)

- Will you ask God for the strength to deny yourself the indulgence of self-pity and self-condemnation?
- How might you better follow Him if you leave behind the inner critic?

Though we walk in the flesh, we are not waging war according to the flesh. For the weapons of our warfare are not of the flesh but have divine power to destroy strongholds. We destroy arguments and every lofty opinion raised against the knowledge of God, and take every thought captive to obey Christ. (2 Corinthians 10:3–5 ESV)

- What specific strongholds do you need divine power to destroy?
- What most recurrent thoughts do you need to take captive, control, and reject?
- How can you rely on God's power, not just on your own?

I have been crucified with Christ. It is no longer I who live, but Christ who lives in me. And the life I now live in the flesh I live by faith in the Son of God, who loved me and gave himself for me. (Galatians 2:20 ESV)

- Can you make Christ welcome at the same time that you welcome self-condemning thoughts and lies?
- In what practical ways can you choose Christ over yourself, your own desires, or your self-condemnation?

> I, I am he who blots out your transgressions for my own sake, and I will not remember your sins. (Isaiah 43:25 ESV)

- What transgressions do you need to surrender as forgiven?
- How might you move past continually remembering what God has forgotten?

Let It Go

Take time to confess to the Lord any past sins that are clinging to your conscience. Accept the forgiveness He offers. Believe He makes strength available to resist repeating those sins. If God does not remember your sins, ask for the faith to forget them and move forward in freedom. Denounce the shame as unworthy of Christ's treasured friend. You may also need to release the real critics who taught you how to be harsh with yourself. Ask God for the grace to blot out the critical messages without despising the messengers.

It is powerful to step into the light of God's Word. It drives out darkness and reveals hidden things. It is like that magnifying mirror on our vanity. We know when we look into it that we are going to see things we would rather not, but without it we would walk around with chin hairs. Sweet sister, let God's Word expose and pluck the unwanted lies, hurts, and shame from your heart, not just today, but often. Self-condemnation has no place in your life. You have this assurance:

> For God so loved the world, that he gave his only Son, that whoever believes in him should not perish but have eternal life. For God did not send his Son into the world to condemn the world,

> but in order that the world might be saved through him. (John 3:16–17 ESV)

Let me put that truth in other words: For God loved you so much that He gave His very own Son to take all condemnation on your behalf, so that if you believe in Him, you are set free from all judgment and will not perish but have everlasting life. God did not send His Son into the world to condemn you for anything, but He came in order that you might be saved through Him.

Do you believe this? That is the most important question you must answer today. Unless you believe that God's Son paid the debt you owe for your rebellion toward God, a debt payable only by death, you are not His friend. In fact, Scripture says you are His enemy. Yet God has done the unthinkable. Consider Paul's words:

> For while we were still weak, at the right time Christ died for the ungodly. . . . God shows his love for us in that while we were still sinners, Christ died for us. Since, therefore, we have now been justified by his blood, much more shall we be saved by him from the wrath of God. For if while we were enemies we were reconciled to God by the death of his Son, much more, now that we are reconciled, shall we be saved by his life. More than that, we also rejoice in God through our Lord Jesus Christ, through whom we have now received reconciliation. (Romans 5:6–11 ESV)

By Christ's great act of friendship, laying down His life for you even while you were an enemy, you who believe can be His friend. No other friendship can make up for the absence of this one. You will never be popular enough, sought after enough, or admired enough to satisfy your desire to be fully known outside of an intimate relationship with God. Striving for more and better friends while rejecting God's friendship is a vain pursuit. Believe and accept what Christ has done for you and He will not only open you to know God's friendship, He will help you know and love yourself. That is the essential first step to knowing and loving others, as Jesus said,

> Love the Lord your God with all your heart and with all your soul and with all your strength and with all your mind; and, Love your neighbor as yourself. (Luke 10:27)

It is time to show yourself some love. It is time to befriend the inner voice and demand that she speak only truth and light. As you let God consistently speak His love and care into your heart through the truth of His Word, I assure you the voice will begin to change.

Years ago, I led a middle-school girls' Sunday school class, and I could see that even at that early age, their inner voices were bullying them. I longed for them to know themselves as God knows them—treasured, pursued, and worthy. The sooner they could settle what was true, the better equipped they would be to resist the lies. I composed this love letter for those girls drawing from the truths God spoke to us in His settled and eternal Word. This is also His love letter to you, His most adored daughter, chosen bride, and intimate friend.

Believe it. Rejoice in it. Rehearse it. Teach it to your inner self.

> Beloved,
>
> My eyes have been on you for as long as I can remember (2 Chronicles 16:9). From the very beginning of time you were destined to be mine (Ephesians 1:5). No other could take your place. I have even written your name on my hand (Isaiah 49:16). You are more valuable to me than a pearl of great price (Matthew 13:45). You are wonderfully made; you need no improvement (Psalm 139:14). I have chosen you from all the others and set you apart (1 Peter 2:9). You are precious in my sight (Isaiah 43:4).
>
> Do not be afraid to love me back (1 John 4:16). I will never disappoint you (Roman 5:8). My love is unfailing (Lamentations 3:32). Nothing can separate you from my love, not any created thing in heaven or on earth (Romans 8:31–39). Even death cannot separate us. I have laid down my life for

you so that we can always be together (John 3:16). My love for you is eternal, without end, for I have loved you with an everlasting love (Jeremiah 31:3).

Should you turn from me, I would pursue you (Luke 15); and when you return, I would rejoice (Isaiah 62:5). My love will cover over all wrongs (Proverbs 10:12). Nothing will come between us because I will never tire of forgiving (Psalm 103).

Delight yourself in my love and I will give you the desires of your heart (Psalm 37:4). I will care for you and give you all you need. I will take away the worries of your heart (Matthew 6:25–34). I will wipe away every tear from your eyes (Revelation 7:17). My riches are abundant and I will give them generously to you (Romans 10:12; Ephesians 3:8). You cannot begin to imagine all that I have prepared especially for you (1 Corinthians 2:9), and I will give you even beyond what you ask. No good thing will I withhold from you (Psalm 84:11). Though you have nothing to offer me in return, I promise to ensure a great inheritance for you (Ephesians 1:14).

All that I desire is that you love me, because I first loved you (1 John 4:19). Love me with all your heart. Love me with all your strength. Love me with your whole mind and your soul (Deuteronomy 6:5). Then all of this will I be free to give you and I will pour my love into your heart (Romans 5:5).

Beloved, be mine.
Jesus

7

This Is Us

The first commentary God gave on relationships was at the beginning of all creation. God looked at the wondrous expression of His glory—the seas, the skies, the vast array of living creatures, and Adam—and He was not satisfied: "It is not good for the man to be alone" (Genesis 2:18).

Aloneness was not God's desire for the singular part of creation that He made in His own image. In yet another of those upside-down realities, God was about to create a shadow on earth that reflects what already exists in fullness in heaven: companionship.

In the earliest disclosure about His own nature, God hinted at something so complex that theologians have never been able to adequately explain it: God lives in companionship as "us." He said, "Let *us* make man in *our* image, after *our* likeness" (Genesis 1:26 ESV, emphasis added). Our understanding of the doctrine of the Trinity, one God in three persons—Father, Son, and Holy Spirit—finds its seed at the beginning of creation and grows page by page as He makes himself known to His friends. It is a confounding, glorious, and mysterious reality for which we have no model here on earth. We have no shadow we can point to in our experience that illuminates how God, who is one, is also three.

Volumes have been written trying to scratch the surface of all the implications of that truth. While we marvel at the mystery of it, one thing is clear: God lives in companionship. It pleased Him to reflect that reality in the image-bearers He created.

> Aloneness was not God's desire for the singular part of creation that He made in His own image.

Even if it were not recorded for us, we know that to be alone is "not good." I'm not saying having alone time is not good. Alone time is catnip for every mother who walked the face of the earth, and probably saved my own children from the wrath of Mom on many occasions. But to be bereft of companionship is literally an unnatural state. It is against the nature of God, and therefore against our nature. We know this to be true when we experience it or even if we only observe it.

One Is a Lonely Number

When my daughter was seven years old, we took an after-school picnic to our local park famous for its pecan trees. The holidays were close and we had plans for those pecans to swim in a delicious chocolate chess pie. It was a beautiful fall Texas day, warm but not hot, a gentle breeze blowing through the branches, making it an ideal day to be outside. Others thought so too. The park was full of mothers with their preschool children, college students playing Frisbee, and couples strolling on the trails.

Hannah and I finished lunch and began to plot our strategy for pecan picking. Trees that dropped their nuts close to the trails had probably already been picked over. Those in the back of the grove were the obvious choice, so those were probably scavenged as well. We chose the trees by the public bathrooms, reasoning the smell would keep all but serious foragers away. After a while we had collected a hefty bag full. A fellow nut-hunter, an older gentleman perhaps in his seventies, stopped to check on our progress.

"You young ladies having any luck?" he asked.

"Yes, sir," Hannah answered. "We have enough to make a pie."

He was impressed with our accomplishment since he had been able to find only a dozen or so himself. We admired his few but large pecans and asked if he came to collect often.

"I like to come here from time to time." Then after a moment he went on. "People ask me what I do to keep busy. Well, I lost my wife seventeen years ago, and I just can't sit inside those four walls day after day. It is just too lonely. So I come out here sometimes to be where people are."

With a sad smile, he shuffled off to search under another tree, alone.

My heart ached for that kind old man. I thought about him in the house where he raised his kids, celebrated anniversaries with his wife, and now sat alone not making more memories, just reliving old ones.

Hannah must have been thinking about him too.

"Mom," she said, "doesn't he have any friends who can visit him? He shouldn't be alone. Let's pray for him."

She was right. He shouldn't be alone. He was being hurt by his loneliness. We stopped picking pecans and asked God to send him comfort and companionship. That's when a voice echoed in my mind: *I did. And you just let him walk away alone.*

We looked up in time to see him getting into his little red pickup and driving off. His loneliness stayed with me long after he was gone, I think because it tapped in to my own fears. I don't want to be alone like that, but what if it happens to me? What if one day I am the person disconnected from meaningful relationships, trying to make a connection with strangers in a park? We fear loneliness because *it is not good for man to be alone.*

The Hebrew word God uses for *man* in that verse is the word that translates *adam*. It can mean a singular man, it can refer to the actual first man created, but it can also mean "mankind." It is the same word God spoke when He said, "Let us make mankind in our image" (Genesis 1:26). God is not simply declaring that it is not good for males to be alone, or for that one male to be alone. The whole counsel of God, with His emphasis on relationships, makes it clear that God was declaring the creatures made in His image, male and female mankind, are not good alone. To bear the image of God demands relationship.

We cannot reflect His "us" image singularly. Only God can do that as the unique Being who is three yet one. And so He completes creation by bringing "one who helps" to be a companion to one who needed to be helped. It is remarkable when you think about the context. Adam was placed in a perfect environment with full provision and meaningful work, yet God declared it "not good" until a human companion was by his side. Yes, she was female, and certainly God would use this unique relationship of male and female for other ordained purposes, but don't miss the blinking billboard that reads HUMAN COMPANIONSHIP REFLECTS THE IMAGE OF GOD!

Our *us-ness* finds realization in marriage, families, nations, communities, and especially friendships. We are less a reflection of our Creator without companionship. Don't misread that. We are not less valuable. We are not less loved. We are not less significant. But God desires that those made in His image enjoy what He enjoys: companionship, oneness, unity. Jesus prayed that God would bring about such intimacy with those who are His friends, that they would "be one, Father, just as you are in me and I am in you. May they also be in us *so that the world may believe that you have sent me*" (John 17:21, emphasis added). God has given us an excess of biblical models to show us how *us-ing* well offers a taste of what He enjoys while also introducing His relational nature to a lonely world.

As the preeminent Friend, we are most like Him when we embrace the role in its particular distinction as "one who helps." God could have made a companion who ruled or one who judged. The companion could have been one who watches, one who follows, one who oversees, or one who directs. Instead, God created *one who helps* after His own image. The psalmist explains,

> God is my helper; the Lord is the upholder of my life. (Psalm 54:4 ESV)

A friend cut in the mold of the Creator is first and foremost one who helps. Self-sufficient as most of us have become, help is now something we expect to hire—not something we seek from very busy friends. So what do we expect from our friends? These days, if you want to know what people think, you ask a focus group. That is what a soda company did. Coca-Cola commissioned a research study to unpack some of the defining characteristics of the current generation in regard to friendships in order to better position their product in the market.

The study, titled "Girl Talk: The New Rules for Female Friendships and Communication," was conducted by the Social Issues Research Center by inquiring of 2,500 respondents, ages twenty-five to thirty-five. This is a partial recounting of their findings. Women reported they want someone who

- will let me be myself;
- can be trusted;
- will be nonjudgmental no matter what;
- will never say, "I told you so";
- will let go of hurt feelings;
- I don't have to explain myself to;
- will be there through thick and thin;
- isn't known as a gossip, but who is good at gossip;
- will keep my secrets but share others' with me.[1]

According to this research, the "average" woman today wants a friend who will make them feel good about themselves, not hold them accountable, be trustworthy to them but willingly disloyal to others, and be devoted in all circumstances. They want an episode of *Friends* or *Sex in the City*. And when they get it, they are often still lonely.

Relationships like this sound shallow and self-serving, but if I am honest, there was a season when that is what I wanted. I thought friends who not only let me be me but also encouraged my own self-focus would fill up the empty places. Of course, they didn't. Because at the root of it, those kinds of relationships are really more about self-love than friend love, about what makes me feel good and look good.

Let's do a little self-examination. What is it you expect from a friend? What do you think she expects from you? Honestly assess your own desires. Ask God to show you your own heart. Don't be embarrassed by what you discover. Truth is a healthy part of rediscovering the lost art of friendship. Get your journal and make your own list.

My Wish List

I've always dreamed of a friend who . . .

The qualities I desire most in a friend are . . .

When it comes to spending time together, I want a friend who . . .

When it comes to taking my side, I want a friend who . . .

If my friend knows I am wrong, choosing unwisely, or settling for sin, I expect . . .

I don't want a friend to interfere in . . .

What I most want to get from my friend is . . .

My best quality as a friend is . . .

The most inconvenient thing about friendship is . . .

What I most want to contribute to my friends is . . .

As you consider your expectations and desires in friendship, ask God to show you how your expectations differ from His vision. Unless you are willing to let go of what you thought you wanted (but has left you lonely and unsatisfied), you will never be able to experience the delights He has prepared.

Greater Expectations

A few years back my husband and I took an empty-nester vacation with a couple we've known since before any of us even built our nests. We were excited to spend time with David and Michelle in the Florida Keys. I love the sand and the sun and expected the white sandy beaches and turquoise blue waters of my dreams. I couldn't wait to arrive.

As we flew over the islands, the scene outside my window took my breath away. The water swirled in varying shades of blues and greens, blending together in a dreamy expanse that extended beyond the horizon. What I couldn't see were those sugar-white beaches. I was disappointed to find that there are very few such beaches in the Keys. Instead, lush vegetation grows almost to the water line, leaving only occasional strips of narrow, gray, mostly manmade beaches blanketed by sulfurous-smelling seaweed.

I couldn't exactly blame the Keys. It was my expectations that were flawed. The Keys simply couldn't provide what I wanted from them. However, in discovering the reason why their beaches were so underwhelming, I discovered something far superior: the Great Florida Reef. It is the only tract of living coral barrier reef in the continental United States, which lies a few miles off the shore of the Keys. It is the cause of the modest beaches and waveless shoreline. It is also the reason the water is so spectacularly clear, creating a wonderland under water. Snorkelers say diving around the reef is like being inside an aquarium. So instead of sitting on a beach watching the waves as I expected, we put on masks and dived into them.

The moment my head went below the water's surface, all sound from above ceased, cutting me off from the known and familiar world. Surrounding me was an environment teeming with life and activity that, remarkably, had been there all along. I leisurely swam with a school of brightly striped fish, as if none of us had any destination in mind. Ten feet below, a large brilliant blue fish scavenged along the coral for a meal. While I could not hear anything from above, I could hear each nibble of the hungry grouper as his lips brushed the reef. A wide variety of ocean life streamed beside, around, and below me in a harmonized ballet of ocean life. I saw rays, barracudas, jellyfish, spiny lobsters, and too many other kinds of fish to describe. I wasn't observing them so much as I felt part of them. No sea critter was startled by my intrusion. Perhaps they assumed I belonged, since I was in their water.

The more I explored, the more wonders I saw. Every moment I experienced an exciting revelation—and even one dangerous one. The first time I crossed over the reef, I saw a shark just thirty feet away. My heart raced and I began to backpedal with my swim fins.

The guide had told us not to worry if we encountered a shark. "They aren't interested in you, so don't freak out."

Internally, I was freaking out. A shark swam in the water with me! I had no experience that informed me what I should do if I was thirty feet from a shark. So I chanted to myself what the instructor had said: "Don't freak out. Don't freak out. Don't freak out." Perhaps the shark's mother had told him the same thing, and he was also playing it cool. Either way, the instructor was right. Neither that shark, nor any of the others I swam with that day, was interested in me. It was a new kind of rejection, but in the end, befriending sharks is probably a bad idea.

The whole adventure was surprising and unexpected. I had not gone to the Keys to snorkel the Great Florida Barrier Reef.

I didn't even know it existed. But once I reconciled that what I expected didn't even exist, I was ready to see and embrace what did. It turned out that the consolation was far better than the beaches I prized.

When we consider how our expectations of friendship—so deeply informed by the culture—have proved to be difficult to fulfill, our first response is naturally disappointment. We have invested years to find meaningful friendships, only to find them unsatisfying. That is the point at which many give up hope for the kind of connection they long to share—the kind that is deeply embedded in our DNA. The problem is not that our longing to be part of "us" relationships is flawed, but that some of our expectations are flawed. It is only in letting go of those old faulty expectations that we discover something that far exceeds them. As we dive into the wonders of biblical, life-giving, life-sharing friendship, we must prepare for a whole new world.

8

What a Girl Wants

We eat out often now that our nest is empty. This frustrates my husband—not because he expects me to cook, but because he knows we will go through the same drill every time:

I can't decide what to order. I send the waiter away twice. When he comes back the third time, I say I'm ready to order, but when he asks what I want, I say, "I'll go last." Then I listen to everyone else order in the hopes that I might hear something that sounds good.

I never know what I want. I know only what I don't want. I don't want anything on the seafood side of the menu—fish stinks. I don't want liver. I don't want spinach. And I'm likely the only Southerner who doesn't want sweet tea.

You would think that narrowing it down would help, but honestly, unless I have a menu with only one thing I like and one thing I don't like, I could be there all day figuring out what to choose. It's the pressure of the waiter poised over me with a pen and everyone at the table staring at me that finally pushes me to just pick the same thing I've had before. At least I know what I'm getting. On those rare occasions I do choose a new dish, I spend the next twenty minutes wondering if I will like it. Sometimes by blind luck I get a dish I love and would order over and over. Most times I end up with food envy, wishing I had what's on my husband's plate. I've even been known to send a disappointing dish back to the kitchen.

How much more enjoyable it would be if the chef would invite me to the kitchen. A sample here, a sample there, and I could be confident in what I order.

I feel like that is where you and I are right now in our journey to deconstruct our friend-life and learn the art of creating something better. We know what we *don't* want: shallow, self-serving, culture-driven friendships. But what *do* we want? This is the point at which we could get stuck. Except, metaphorically speaking, we have been invited into the kitchen to see the very best recipe for friendship being put together.

The entire Bible, from Adam to Jesus, spells out the ingredients, the techniques, and even the spiritual health benefits involved in creating meaningful, lasting, God-modeled relationships. That is by no means to say we can attain perfect friendships. We won't ever be able to re-create the wonderful dish of friendship God himself serves up, but we can have fewer relationships that we want to send back. With a new vision, we won't even have friend-envy, wishing we had the relationships others have found.

So what is on the menu? Let me list some aspects of life-sharing friendship that I hope make you hungry for more than you have enjoyed before. All of these have been modeled by real people in real-life relationships and recorded in Scripture as a recipe for us to follow. A life-sharing friend is one who

- is loyal in every circumstance.
- will make personal sacrifices for you.
- makes you wiser.
- fills the gaps of your weaknesses.
- helps you get rid of things that keep you from God.

- is never jealous and does not compete with you.
- always settles differences with reconciliation.
- is committed to your development.
- can be trusted without reservations.
- holds you accountable but without judgment.
- hears your fears and lends you courage.
- cheers when you find other friends.
- is transparent and honest.
- shares her innermost thoughts and feelings.
- respects your individuality.
- respects your boundaries.
- joins you in hardship.
- will be your partner.
- takes action when you need it most.
- stirs your longing for godliness.
- can take a rebuke with grace and appreciation.
- can give a rebuke with gentleness and love.
- loves and expects nothing in return.

Call it a smorgasbord. Call it a feast. Call it biblical life-sharing friendship that exemplifies how God is our friend. We will never experience from each other the fullness of this kind of friendship any more than I could duplicate Julia Child's signature dish. But girl, now we know! This is what we want! Better a slightly overcooked beef bourguignon than a bologna sandwich. God has set before us a menu from a five-star Michelin restaurant. Will we really choose to stick with Oscar Mayer because it is what we have come to expect? Of course not. We want the wonderful, satisfying flavors of friendship that have been seasoned by the masterful hand of God.

In chapter 10 we will look at the specific biblical examples that illustrate the life-sharing aspects of friendship I listed above. First, though, spend time asking God to stir a hunger within you so full of anticipation that you will be unsatisfied to settle ever again for the cold leftovers the culture has been serving.

Lord, make your desire for friendship my desire.

First in Line

As with every good meal, the time will come when you must pay the bill. The better the food, the higher the price. Here is where you find out what this new and wonderful feast of friendship will cost you.

> It goes like this—to have an exceptional friend, you have to be an exceptional friend. Don't bother pursuing these life-giving, life-sharing relationships unless you are willing first to serve up the same.

It will cost *your* friendship. Unless you are willing to pay that price, you better get used to bologna sandwiches. In fact, to enjoy what you have just seen on the menu, you actually have to pay before you receive. It goes like this—to have an exceptional friend, you have to be an exceptional friend. Don't bother pursuing these life-giving, life-sharing relationships unless you are willing first to serve up the same. That is the model. God was our friend *first*. "We love because he first loved us" (1 John 4:19).

From Adam to Paul, God made the first friendship move. He initiated. He loved. He pursued. He sacrificed. Remember again that friendship isn't just something nice to have. It is our calling. To live a friend-life worthy of our calling, we follow in His footsteps. Jesus reminds us, "You did not choose me, but I chose you and appointed you so that you might go and bear fruit—fruit that will last—so that whatever you ask in my name the Father will give you" (John 15:16).

In one of Jesus' most intimate and humble acts of friendship, He stripped off His outer garments, knelt on the floor (taking a servant's role), and washed His friends' feet. His actions were shocking to them. He was the Teacher, the leader of their group of friends. Imagine the Queen of England setting aside her crown and slipping on an apron and cap to serve dinner to her butler, cook, and lady's maid. Awkward! Jesus' humbling himself before His friends was far more awkward and uncomfortable than any such earthly humility. It was so uncomfortable that one friend tried to stop Him.

> Jesus knew on the evening of Passover Day that it would be his last night on earth before returning to his Father. . . . Jesus knew that the Father had given him everything and that he had come from God and would return to God. And how he loved his disciples! So, he got up from the supper table, took off his robe, wrapped a towel around his loins, poured water into a basin, and began to wash the disciples' feet and to wipe them with the towel he had around him. When he came to Simon Peter, Peter said to him, "Master, you shouldn't be washing our feet like this!"
>
> Jesus replied, "You don't understand now why I am doing it; some day you will."
>
> "No," Peter protested, "you shall never wash my feet!"
>
> "But if I don't, you can't be my partner," Jesus replied.
>
> Simon Peter exclaimed, "Then wash my hands and head as well—not just my feet!"
>
> Jesus replied, "One who has bathed all over needs only to have his feet washed to be entirely clean. Now you are clean—but that isn't true of everyone here." For Jesus knew who would betray him. That is what he meant when he said, "Not all of you are clean."
>
> After washing their feet he put on his robe again and sat down and asked, "Do you understand what I was doing? You call me 'Master' and 'Lord,' and you do well to say it, for it is true. And since I, the Lord and Teacher, have washed your feet, you ought to wash each other's feet. I have given you an example to follow: do as I have done to you. How true it is that a servant is not greater than his master. Nor is the messenger more important than the

> one who sends him. You know these things—now do them! That is the path of blessing. (John 13:1–17 TLB)

Serving first. Loving first. Friending first. That is the path to blessing. It satisfied Jesus not to be served by His friends, but to serve them. All of them. Even the friend He knew doubted Him and was betraying Him. No passive-aggressive comments. He didn't wait for Judas to leave first. He was a friend to him too.

Jesus could serve in this way because His confidence did not come from what these friends thought of Him. He did not find worth in how much they wanted to be His friend. He didn't like them because they liked Him. He could humble himself in servile friendship, acting first, because His confidence was in His true identity. *Jesus knew that the Father had given Him everything and that He had come from God and would return to God.*

Beloved sister, without a sense of your true identity, you will be susceptible to wrong motives in your friendships with others. You will fear their judgment or crave their approval. You will wait for them to act in friendship first because insecurity is paralyzing. But lookee here—you can say with confidence almost the same thing Jesus said: *I know that the Father has given me everything and that I was created by God and will return to God.*

What is the *everything* He has given you? Well, how about all the riches of heaven, His pleasure, everything you need for enjoyment, a divine calling to be His child, purpose, full access to His very throne, spiritual power in the heavenly realms, and a secure eternal future with Him. Peter summed it up this way:

> His divine power has given us everything we need for a godly life through our knowledge of him who called us by his own glory and goodness. (2 Peter 1:3)

Most especially, *everything* includes His friendship. He likes you. One of the most iconic moments in Academy Awards history came from actress Sally Field's acceptance speech. She was so overwhelmed by the recognition that she famously exclaimed, "You like me! Right now, you like me!" It was a transparent moment that revealed she hadn't been sure how her peers felt about her. She was flabbergasted by the evidence that they actually liked her.

We have evidence that God really likes us. He didn't just give us a meaningless award. He gave us the life of His Son!

He doesn't just like you—He loves you! You can risk offering your friendship to others because you have the most meaningful friendship you cannot lose. You are secure! That means you can friend like Jesus: sacrificially, humbly, and joyfully. His kind of friendship, while given first and without strings or expectations, is so winsome, so compelling, so appetizing, it often inspires loyal affection in return. Jesus' friends were so won by His love that all but one committed their lives to serving Him, even to the point of death.

Investing in your friends will most certainly cost comfort, convenience, intimacy, time, money, prayer, pride, patience, and a hundred other costs you will discover. But you won't get bologna!

This might be a good time to look again at that menu. Is this what you really want? Do you really want to experience friendship in the image of God? Investing in your friends will most certainly cost comfort, convenience, intimacy, time, money, prayer, pride, patience, and a hundred other costs you will discover. But you won't get bologna! The cost of friendship brings the most wonderful comfort dish you could ever imagine—authentic, intimate companionship. How great that you get the privilege of serving it to others first.

9

Till Death Do Us Part

Like most moms, in sentimental fashion I saved all my kids' favorites books from years gone by. As toddlers, one they begged to hear over and over was simply titled *Mine*. The story featured the beloved characters and best friends from *Sesame Street* Bert and Ernie, only as toddler versions of themselves. In the book, the characters Little Bert and Little Ernie can't get along because they are too greedy to share their favorite toys. Page after page, the Muppet friends clutch their own toys and declare "Mine!" when asked to share. One or the other is left out while the possessor enjoys the spoils of ownership.

As the mom of toddlers, that was a familiar scene. I hoped reading the book would help my little ones see the value of sharing. Instead, as I turned the pages, my kids were always chanting along merrily with the naughty Muppets, "Mine, mine, mine!"

I wasn't surprised. One of the first words most of us learn is that self-centered exclamation. It comes from our very human nature that tells us to hoard every good thing lest someone take it away. It may start inconsequentially with wanting the best crayons, but left untempered, the seeds of greed grow as we grow. "Mine, mine, mine" in a child can mature into "me, me, me" as an adult—and there is nothing more unattractive than a spoiled and greedy grown-up. I know, because I became one—at least when it came to one friendship. Looking back, I see it now as plainly as I could see Bert holding back his favorite fire truck from Ernie, but at the time I only saw that I was about to lose something I thought was mine. In response to my fear, I essentially said, "Fine, I don't want to play anymore."

I was sitting on the front porch of our home one beautiful spring day when I told a most beloved and treasured friend, "I think it would be best if we didn't pursue our friendship going forward."

It was one of the most difficult conversations I've ever had. I was telling someone I loved and enjoyed and desperately wanted in my life that we shouldn't spend time together. I had convinced myself I was being mature and noble, but in hindsight, I was being selfish and petulant because I didn't know how to share.

I wasn't good at girl relationships, which I think we have established. She, on the other hand, seemed adept at the art of friending. Everyone wanted to be her friend. So many that I felt as though I was in a competition. I didn't like the jealousy and insecurity it brought out in me. I was like Bert, pouting and clinging to the thing someone wanted to take away. I had never been a jealous person, and I knew I couldn't keep it up. Too many Ernies wanted to share my friend, and every one left me feeling threatened. I had to set boundaries—which, in fact, were walls.

By rejecting the friendship, I thought I would spare myself the hurt, but I just walled it in with me. The insecurities were not about her. They were about me—but I had yet to learn that. Over the years, as I watched that friend's relationships grow and expand to include even more people, I felt the loss over and over again. Why didn't she choose me over them? Why couldn't I make it work?

Today, of course, I know why. I wanted her to be my exclusive BFF, focusing on what *I* needed from the friendship. I was screaming "mine, mine, mine" when I should have been wondering what she also needed from our friendship. I should have taken turns and been willing to share this awesome woman so others could gain from knowing her as I did. You cannot fear something will be taken from you if you freely give it away. It was a hard and humbling lesson. I will always be sorry I didn't have the maturity back then to salvage our friendship. Yet at the same time, it was relationship failures like that one that made me examine my insecurities and deal with them. It was also the catalyst I needed to do some Bible sleuthing to discover the all-important ingredients necessary for hearty friendships. Unless those made in God's image are willing to take His instruction, they will never find truly satisfying relationships. His Word is the guide for what makes eternally significant, soul-enriching friendships. Spoiler alert: Jealousy is not on the list.

Looking for a Forever Friend

The classic *Anne of Green Gables* by L. M. Montgomery follows the life of an enchanting and quirky orphan named Anne, who ends up the ward of two elderly unmarried siblings. While it is a coming-of-age story, it is also an exploration of the life-giving power of friendship. We get a hint this will be its theme from an early scene, when Anne, still in an orphanage, is so desperate to be known and loved that she befriends her own reflection in a window.

What she really wants more than anything in the world is a bosom friend. She explains it this way: "A bosom friend—an intimate friend, you know—a really kindred spirit to whom I can confide my innermost soul. I've dreamed of meeting her all my life."[1]

Those words resonate in human hearts made in God's image. We crave that kind of intimate connection. We don't all articulate it as well as Anne, but when we discover it, we know that is what we wanted all along. Anne found the connection her soul was longing for in Diana, a young classmate who was steady as a rock even when outshined by Anne. One vulnerable and brave moment bonded them forever.

"Oh, Diana," said Anne at last, clasping her hands and speaking almost in a whisper, "oh, do you think you can like me a little—enough to be my bosom friend?"

Diana laughed. Diana always laughed before she spoke. "Why, I guess so," she said frankly. "I'm awfully glad you've come to live at Green Gables. It will be jolly to have somebody to play with. There isn't any other girl who lives near enough to play with, and I've no sisters big enough."

"Will you swear to be my friend forever and ever?" demanded Anne eagerly.

Diana looked shocked. "Why it's dreadfully wicked to swear," she said rebukingly.

"Oh no, not my kind of swearing. There are two kinds, you know."

"I never heard of but one kind," said Diana doubtfully.

"There really is another. Oh, it isn't wicked at all. It just means vowing and promising solemnly."

"Well, I don't mind doing that," agreed Diana, relieved. "How do you do it?"

"We must join hands—so," said Anne gravely. "It ought to be over running water. We'll just imagine this path is running water. I'll repeat the oath first. I solemnly swear to be faithful to my bosom friend, Diana Barry, as long as the sun and moon shall endure. Now you say it and put my name in."

Diana repeated the "oath" with a laugh fore and aft. Then she said: "You're a queer girl, Anne. I heard before that you were queer. But I believe I'm going to like you real well."[2]

So began the start of a beautiful friendship, but it was just the start. Anne and Diana would face all the challenges of life and young adulthood together, building on something significant: their oath. So many wonderful aspects of true friendship are brought to life in that book, not the least of which is *covenant friendship.* "Will you swear to be my friend forever and ever?" Anne asked.

A covenant is more than just a contract. An attorney will tell you that a contract can be broken. A covenant, on the other hand, is a pledge you make and (here is the kicker) that remains in effect even if one of the parties breaks it.

When it comes to biblically patterned friendships, Anne got it right. They are relationships meant to last "as long as the sun and moon shall endure." Covenant friendship is what God enters into with us—an unbreakable pledge He will keep no matter what. Paul described it this way: "If we are faithless, he remains faithful—for he cannot deny himself" (2 Timothy 2:13).

If God were to break His pledge of friendship to us, one He sealed at the cross, that would be tantamount to denying himself. He cannot deny himself, and so we have this confidence: "He who did not spare his own Son, but gave him up for us all—how will he not also, along with him, graciously give us all things?" (Romans 8:32).

When we commit to biblically patterned friendship, like Anne, and more so like Jesus, we are not just making an agreement to be nice to someone as long as she is nice to us. Or to meet each other's needs as long as we find it convenient or while we live in the same town. We are entering into a covenant that unites us and calls us to be faithful helpers to the very end. To do less would actually mean to deny ourselves.

A friendship that has always inspired me in this scope of faithfulness is not a storybook tale, but the real-life relationship of two guys from vastly different life stations. Jonathan was born to privilege. David was born to work in the pasture. When their stories intersected, they found in each other a kindred spirit in whom to confide their innermost souls. Their story, recorded in the books of Samuel, teach many friendship lessons that are patterned after the original.

David and Jonathan: A Covenant Friendship

Jonathan was by birth a man of rank and consequence. He was the eldest son of Saul, the first king of Israel, a sovereign appointed by God himself. Not only was Jonathan in line to succeed his father, he was a fierce soldier and war hero. His reputation for courage and wisdom was well established, and the nation looked with assurance to the royal line of succession. He was a man of confidence and purpose, who was rising to the call of his duties.

One day, he went to his father's court to hear a young man named David share details of how he felled a giant Philistine warrior with a stone from his slingshot. The youth was standing before the king, giving testimony to how he stood against Israel's enemy who dared to defy the living God. How unexpected it must have been for the king and court to hear this amazing young guy admit he was the son of Jesse, a mere farmer in the king's realm. This package of courage wrapped up in humility caught the attention of the king's son. Perhaps it was because Jonathan had those same qualities and so felt an instant kinship, and a friendship began. In fact, "the soul of Jonathan was knit to the soul of David and Jonathan loved him as himself" (1 Samuel 18:1 NASB).

With David now ensconced in the royal court at Saul's pleasure, Jonathan committed fully to his friendship with David. "Then Jonathan made a covenant with David, because he loved him as his own soul. And Jonathan stripped himself of the robe that was on him and gave it to David, and his armor, and even his sword and his bow and his belt" (1 Samuel 18:3–4 ESV).

This was a big deal in so many ways. Jonathan wasn't just sharing his favorite T-shirt. He was basically giving David his position. Jonathan was a commander of armies. Jonathan wore the robes of the heir to the kingdom. Instead of being jealous that his father and the whole kingdom were lauding another man, Jonathan lauded him too. In fact, he was already realizing that David had a calling on his life. From the beginning of their relationship it seems Jonathan had decided to help David fulfill that calling and not hinder it—even if it came at a personal cost to him.

It takes uncommon strength of character and spiritual maturity to meet the biblical high calling of friendship. Jesus said to love others as we love ourselves, but then He demonstrated something even greater, which Paul later called us to strive toward: "Do nothing from selfish ambition or conceit, but in humility count others more significant than yourselves" (Philippians 2:3 ESV).

Jonathan loved David *more* than himself. How easy it is to get jealous of our friends. On the one hand, we want them to succeed and prosper. On the other hand, when they do, we can feel envious and even left behind. Jonathan, though, knew the cure for the green-flu—humble love. Not just any degree of love, but loving as he loved himself, and then a measure beyond that. To love to that extent meant that promoting David was like promoting himself, and wounding David would be wounding himself. Jonathan could essentially concede David's superiority and give deference to his best good without feeling cheated.

It was Saul who began to burn with jealousy as David accrued victory upon victory on the battlefield. Even though David did all for the honor of the king, Saul turned murderous. When Saul called Jonathan in to tell him that he wanted David killed, Jonathan chose loyalty to his friend and warned David. He sent him to hide and promised to advocate for him before his father, which he did.

> Jonathan spoke well of David to Saul his father and said to him, "Let not the king sin against his servant David, because he has not sinned against you, and because his deeds have brought good to you. For he took his life in his hand and he struck down the Philistine, and the LORD worked a great salvation for all Israel. You saw it, and rejoiced. Why then will you sin against innocent blood by killing David without cause?" And Saul listened to the voice of Jonathan. Saul swore, "As the LORD lives, he shall not be put to death." And Jonathan called David, and Jonathan reported to him all these things. And Jonathan brought David to Saul, and he was in his presence as before. (1 Samuel 19:4–7 ESV)

In the model of the Lord, Jonathan was the advocate interceding for his friend. I don't think any of my friends will ever need me to stand between them and an earthly sovereign, but there are ways we advocate for our friends. We stand in the gap in prayer for them before a heavenly Sovereign. That is no small thing. Our Sovereign has not just the power of life and death, but power over this world and the one we cannot see. To pray for them is to stand at the throne and ask for mercy or grace or both. We also advocate for them when we speak the truth about them, especially before those who do not. We advocate when we promote reconciliation in their lives and when we seek their spiritual prosperity.

Jonathan would do this again and again for David as his father became more and more unhinged by fear and jealousy. The truth had become clear: God intended to remove leadership from Saul. Saul's sins had disqualified him as God's anointed leader, and it was now David—not Jonathan—whom God chose to succeed him. With Saul raging at his son for not betraying David, the king bluntly laid out the consequences:

> "For as long as the son of Jesse lives on the earth, neither you nor your kingdom shall be established. Therefore, send and bring him to me, for he shall surely die." Then Jonathan answered Saul his father, "Why should he be put to death? What has he done?" But Saul hurled his spear at him to strike him. So Jonathan knew that his father was determined to put David to death. And Jonathan rose from the table in fierce anger and ate no food the second day of the month, for he was grieved for David, because his father had disgraced him. (1 Samuel 20:31–34 ESV)

Fully counting the cost, Jonathan reckoned that it was better to be David's friend than to be a king. Ruminate on that for a moment. Jonathan reckoned that it was better to be a friend than a king. Jonathan was also saying it was better to be a friend than wealthy. It was better to be a friend than indulge his father. It was better to be a friend than have prestige and power. It was better to be a friend than have fame.

This, my dear friend-hungry girlfriend, is what it means to show love by laying down your life. The Greek word for "lay down" (*tithémi*) that Jesus used to call us to ultimate friendship doesn't just mean *to forfeit*. It also means *to lay aside*. Consider Jonathan's actions this way: *Greater love has no man than he would lay aside the cares and ambitions of his own life for his friend* (see John 15:13).

Greater love lays aside our comforts for the comfort of a friend. It lays aside our ambitions if we can promote the ambitions of a friend. It lays aside personal needs to meet the needs of a friend. For Jonathan, it was laying aside his legitimate expectation of being king so that David could answer the call God had on his life. What does that look like in your friendships or potential friendships today?

It's better to be a friend than ________.

Better than what? You probably won't have to give up a throne, but are you willing to lay aside other things that could come between you and a friend's best good? Is it better to be a friend than *right*? Is it better to be a friend than *being first*? Is it better to be a friend than *being popular*? Is it better to be a friend than *to be in charge*? Is it better to be a friend than *having more money*? Is it better to be a friend than *to be unburdened*?

Our friendships will always be stifled as long as we value something more than being a friend. Covenant friendship, cut from God-cloth, expects we will be willing to lay aside self-interest for the benefit, encouragement, and help of a friend because in humility, we not only grow to love them as ourselves, but we count others more significant than ourselves.

What you do for your friend, in essence, you do for yourself, because a covenant friend is part of you.

Friending is getting very real—and seemingly costly. But here is something Jonathan knew: When you love like this, you are ultimately sacrificing for part of yourself. The "us" factor brings your sacrifice back to you. What you do for your friend, in essence, you do for yourself, because a covenant friend is part of you. Only when you put that to the test will you experience the unexpected satisfaction that comes from not satisfying yourself first. Upside-down crazy, right?

It must have seemed crazy to Saul. He tried to kill his own son because of the loyalty Jonathan showed to David. The messiness of the situation meant it was best for David and Jonathan to part ways. With embraces and tears (manly tears, I'm sure), Jonathan gave a final blessing to his dear friend whom he did not expect to see again:

> "Go in peace, because we have sworn both of us in the name of the LORD, saying, 'The LORD shall be between me and you, and between my offspring and your offspring, forever.'" And he rose and departed, and Jonathan went into the city. (1 Samuel 20:42 ESV)

Jonathan revealed the key ingredient that transforms a friendship of convenience into a covenant relationship: "The LORD shall be between me and you." When any friendship is a cord of three strands with the Lord between, it is a relationship that goes the distance of forever. That is how long Jonathan and David pledged their loyalty to each other. They did so with God as the third in their intimate circle. Jonathan was not just investing in temporary camaraderie. He was laying up the treasure of friendship in heaven where he would one day pick it up. His sights were set far into the future.

Are you patiently developing farsighted friendships, or are you content with nearsighted pals? A nearsighted view settles for having a friend you can take girl trips with or someone who will travel with you through motherhood. They are relationships that strive only to meet your current felt needs. You might become nearsighted because you relocate frequently and it seems like too much effort to make temporary friends. You get nearsighted when you have a cut-and-run view that says it is okay to end a friendship when it is no longer easy, convenient, or rewarding. None of those are biblical, life-sharing, covenant friendships.

That is not because they focus on the need of today—our friendships should absolutely meet us where we are and give us joy, fun, and support. They fall short because they are *only* about today. We are called to God's pattern, which is a promise to love and keep loving despite what brings about distance, disappointment, or seasonal disinterest. Jonathan knew that his friendship with David would one day reach to the full expanse of heaven's gates. Our relationships can too. One day we will pick up where we left off with all those relationships when we said, "The Lord shall be between you and me." Better to be a friend through trials, hard seasons, and distance than to be a *lonely skeptic.*

Go and linger in the story in 1 Samuel 18–20. Three times they renewed their covenant to each other. They shared their sorrows, bore each other's burdens, consoled and counseled each other, sought God together, spurred each other on to faithfulness, shared feelings, and kept confidences. Theirs was a mature and mutual friendship. You will notice that Jonathan carried the greater burden of being the one who helped. This, too, we can expect.

Is it really possible that a friendship can be measure-for-measure equal in sacrifice? God's friendship is one of bearing the greater burden. And when a friendship has us doing the heavy lifting as the one who helps, that is when we are most like Him. Cast in that image, Jonathan kept his integrity by not keeping account on a balance sheet. While the help might not have been measure for measure, their love and commitment certainly were.

Given the opportunity to kill Saul, who had been hunting David mercilessly, he showed mercy to his friend's father and the man God had anointed king. His love for Jonathan and God was stronger than any desire for revenge. David refused to wrestle the crown from Saul or Jonathan even though God had anointed him the next king. For David, it was also better to be a friend than to be king. God would have a time and a method for crowning David that did not require betraying his friend.

When Saul and Jonathan eventually died on the battlefield at the hand of Israel's enemies, David carried nothing but grief in his heart. Though he grieved Saul, who missed every opportunity to reconcile, he especially grieved his friend.

"Jonathan lies slain on your high places. I am distressed for you, my brother Jonathan; very pleasant have you been to me; your love to me was extraordinary, surpassing the love of women. How the mighty have fallen, and the weapons of war perished!" (2 Samuel 1:26–27 ESV).

Jonathan, as a friend, was a mighty person in David's life, and David well knew it. He loved Jonathan and would continue to fulfill their covenant even after Jonathan's death. After David ascended to the throne, he discovered that one of Jonathan's sons, Mephibosheth, had survived the national unrest. The young man, crippled in both feet, would benefit from David's forever-covenant of friendship to his father, receiving an inheritance and also becoming David's friend.

David said to him, "Do not fear, for I will show you kindness for the sake of your father Jonathan, and I will restore to you all the land of Saul your father, and you shall eat at my table always" (2 Samuel 9:7 ESV).

Take some time to ask God for insights into any fledgling or struggling relationships.

- Have you invited God to be between you and the other friend have committed yourself to?
- Are you willing to make that invitation to Him directly and invite your friend to do the same?
- What might adopting a covenant mind-set change in a current friendship?
- In what ways have your relationships been hindered because you love yourself more than your friends?
- Is there a place God is prompting you to lay aside your life and consider the other person and her needs as more significant than your own?
- Think again of Jonathan and David's example. How is God speaking to your heart about artfully friending in such ways?

10

Service with a Smile

"There was a man in the land of Uz whose name was Job . . ." So began his fateful story. Job was like the awesome guy in church who has lots of money and success, but we would never know it by his demeanor. He was a good ol' boy who was fair to his employees, loved his wife and kids, and was generous with what he had. He was the last guy you'd expect to have a downturn, but that was exactly what happened. Through no fault of his own, he lost his wealth, his kids, his health, and his reputation. Isn't losing any of those our biggest fear? Money is our security. Kids are our pride. Health lets us enjoy all that we have. Reputation is the very heart of our self-identity. Losing any one of those could cause the strongest to falter. Losing them all? Who could withstand such desolation? Job certainly did not think he could and said as much.

> He spoke up and cursed his fate: "Obliterate the day I was born. Blank out the night I was conceived! Let it be a black hole in space. May God above forget it ever happened. Erase it from the books! . . . Why does God bother giving light to the miserable, why bother keeping bitter people alive. Those who want in the worst way to

> die, and can't, who can't imagine anything better than death, who count the day of their death and burial the happiest day of their life? What's the point of life when it doesn't make sense, when God blocks all the roads to meaning? . . . The worst of my fears has come true, what I've dreaded most has happened. My repose is shattered, my peace destroyed. No rest for me, ever—death has invaded life" (Job 3:2–3, 20–23, 25–26 *The Message*).

Have you felt that way? More to the point of our quest to be a friend, what do you say to someone who feels that way?

Whenever we hear a story, our initial reaction is to project ourselves onto the protagonist. We see ourselves as Job. We know what it is to feel loss and hopelessness. Job, though, is not the friend in this story. He is the one who needs a friend's help. Our lessons come from those around him.

A Dash of Silence

We get two flavors of friendship in the early experience of Job's crisis. The first is seasoned by his wife, who looks at Job's pathetic circumstances and cannot believe he still reveres his God, who would allow such suffering. In all the ruin, Job refused to accuse his Maker, declaring, "The LORD gave and the LORD has taken away; may the name of the LORD be praised" (Job 1:21).

Rather than encouraging his declaration of trust, Mrs. Job offers advice that points him away from God. "Are you still maintaining your integrity? Curse God and die!" (Job 2:9).

She is the friend who shows up when you are going through hard things and helps you throw yourself a pity party. Mistaking commiserating for support, she reinforces hurt, bitterness, and complaint. Her comments always leave you feeling more justified in your misery than comforted, more victimized than victor, and more hopeless than encouraged. Well-meaning or not, the hole you are in will be deeper thanks to this friend's words of "support."

It is after she serves up a heaping helping of bitterroot onto Job's plate that Job utters those curses on his own life. In contrast, consider the second, more palatable flavor of friendship served to Job. This dish was a sweet support from friends who traveled to be with him in his crisis.

> Three of Job's friends heard of all the trouble that had fallen on him. Each traveled from his own country—Eliphaz from Teman, Bildad from Shuhah, Zophar from Naamath—and went together to Job to keep him company and comfort him. When they first caught sight of him, they couldn't believe what they saw—they hardly recognized him! They cried out in lament, ripped their robes, and dumped dirt on their heads as a sign of their grief. Then they sat with him on the ground. Seven days and nights they sat there without saying a word. They could see how rotten he felt, how deeply he was suffering. (Job 2:11–13 *The Message*)

Consider the picture of God-friendship these three displayed. They were not too busy to be attentive to what was going on in their friend's life. They came near, even at great inconvenience. They took the pain of their friend on themselves, giving him space to grieve and lament, and also joining him in it. They did not compound his crisis with false assurances or indignant declarations. Their presence was their comfort. Their silence was their help.

That sounds simple, but most of us default quickly to words. And sometimes the less we know what to say, the more we seem to ramble. What words will make it better? Unfortunately, words untimely spoken often make things worse. Proverbs 29:11 says, "A fool gives full vent to his spirit, but a wise man quietly holds it back" (ESV). It is a wise friend who can exercise restraint and give God room in the silence.

Another default response is to act quickly. *What can I do to make it better?* I am a fixer, so I resemble this response. It was an honest friend who once told me, "Kim, I don't need you to find a solution. I just need you to listen." That rebuke has served our friendship well. It also led to some insights about myself. I love to help, but thanks to my friend's honesty, I came to adopt a personal mantra: *Help not asked for is interference*. Consider that a bonus if this speaks to your struggle too.

While misplaced actions and words are foolish, "a word fitly spoken is like apples of gold in a setting of silver" (Proverbs 25:11 ESV). That is something Job's friends had not mastered. They didn't know when to speak or what to say. When they eventually did engage him with words, they proved to be unwise and drew a rebuke from God. Their friendship demonstrates that intentional companionable silence can help more effectively than a thousand misguided words. When they helped with the power of their presence and unrushed silent solidarity, they friended unselfishly. The solace of shared tears and the consolation of intimacy served in wordless restraint became comfort food to a desolate friend.

- Who needs your silent strength?
- In what ways can you friend powerfully with your nearness?
- What words do you need to hold back to give space?
- Who needs the solidarity of your tears?

These are essential ingredients of mature, spiritual, life-giving friendship. Instead of thinking about how to get this kind of support from others, our journey of friendship starts with seeking how to give it. Take time to process the implications of offering yourself this way.

- In what ways would this kind of friendship be difficult for you to express?
- When have you been on the receiving end? What was the impact?
- How have you experienced God meeting you in these ways?

- In what ways can you be sure that the words you speak are grounded in biblical wisdom?
- In what ways do you need to grow in maturity and patience to be present with those who need your silent strength and the compassion to truly share in their troubles?

More Ingredients

No two relationships are the same, but there are common ingredients we all need for a balanced dish of friendship: confidentiality, honesty, courtesy, respect, compassion, boundaries, and counsel—just to name a few. Every relationship will offer a unique blend, but no relationship can be healthy if essential ingredients are left out altogether. Imagine a friend who offers up a huge spoonful of honesty but not an ounce of compassion or respect. Oh, the difference just a spoonful of sugar can make when consuming something bitter.

When my young daughter was first testing her skills in the kitchen, I suggested she try no-bake cookies. Seven ingredients and a little heat from the microwave should have been a no-fail recipe, but Hannah got distracted. With her friend there to "help" and divert her, they didn't remember what they had already tossed into the bowl. It wasn't until they served the cookies that it was obvious what was missing—sugar. Instead of measuring out a cup of sugar, they added a cup of salt. They made everyone taste their creation before realizing their mistake. We were a house of sourpusses, and none of us was sure we wanted to taste their second try.

Friendships go sour when essential ingredients are left out, but we don't have the luxury of tossing out ruined relationships to start again. If that were to happen, you can be sure that others would see that you handle friendships carelessly. If that is your habit, you shouldn't be surprised to find few eager to taste your next attempt. Instead, entice others to "taste and see" what you have to offer by incorporating the very best makings of biblical covenant friendship—the ones on the menu we browsed in chapter 8. We are not just receivers of all those great dishes. We should also be serving them up to others.

Our family has experience when it comes to learning to be good servers. Each of our three sons worked as a waiter during their college years. The upside of their employment was getting a little parental payback. It was priceless to have my children wait on me—and to have to do it with a smile.

> Friendships go sour when essential ingredients are left out.

The first time our younger son, Bailey, served us, he stood there, gainfully employed, in his crisp white shirt and clean black apron, and asked if he could take my drink order. It was both an emotional and delicious experience. Of course, my happiness paled in comparison to his sister's joy at being able to send her brother back to the kitchen for more sour cream, extra chips, a drink refill, or more napkins. Her favorite taunt was to ask him to recite the daily specials.

"Tell me about the shrimp again."

"What kind of sauces does that have?"

"Can I get that with green sauce instead of cream sauce?"

"How do they make their guacamole?"

To her delight—and his frustration—he could (and had to!) answer all of her questions. You see, to be a server, he had to know about every dish. Before he was even hired, he had to pass a test about the menu and all the "extras" the restaurant offers. The very best servers are the ones who know the ins and outs of the menu.

Girl, we are the servers. We have the honor of serving up the very best qualities of friendship. If we don't know what those qualities are, if we have not understood them as God designed, how can we serve them to others? Preparation is a key ingredient of friendship. Certainly, we have instincts that point us in the right direction, but God invites us to become experts. Make a plan to spend time learning from the friends whose stories God has preserved. Not only will you discover what is most appetizing to you, but as you learn, you will grow to be the friend others come back to again and again for the unique taste of heaven you serve up.

Serving Suggestions

Jonathan and David's friendship and the relationship of Job to his three friends are just two of many God-patterned friendship stories in the Bible. Many others give us the chance to see imperfect people as they strove to follow a perfect pattern. Each one encourages us to embrace our human frailties and aim high anyway.

Find some time to thoughtfully and prayerfully read their stories. Ask God to give you insights that can help as you imperfectly live out His example in your own unique story. I've included a guide to some of those stories to get you started.

- Make a goal to read one friendship story a week from the menu below.
- Start with *The Dish* that is most appetizing to you.
- Focus on areas you would like to develop in your own life.
- Keep a journal to record the lessons and the principles of friendship you discover.
- Ask God how you might serve up those principles in your specific relationships.
- Don't stress about conquering this list. Take your time and savor each example of biblical friendship in action.

The Dish	The Servers
A friend who shares her innermost thoughts and feelings.	God and Adam (Genesis 1–3)
A friend who respects your individuality.	God and Adam (Genesis 3)
A friend who is transparent and honest.	God and Abraham (Genesis 16)

The Dish	The Servers
A friend who fills the gap of your weaknesses.	Moses and Aaron (Exodus 4)
A friend who hears your fears and lends you courage.	Joshua, Caleb, and the spies (Numbers 13)
A friend who takes action when you need it most.	Ruth and Naomi (Ruth 1–4)
A friend who will make personal sacrifices for you.	Jonathan and David (1 Samuel 18–20)
A friend who can take a rebuke with grace and appreciation.	David and Nathan (2 Samuel 12)
A friend who is loyal in every circumstance.	Elijah and Elisha (2 Kings 2)
A friend who stirs your longing for godliness.	Shadrach, Meshach, and Abed-nego (Daniel 6)
A friend who holds you accountable but without judgment.	Jesus and Peter (Matthew 16)
A friend whom you can trust without reservations.	Elizabeth and Mary (Luke 1)
A friend who can give a rebuke with gentleness and love.	Jesus and Martha (Luke 10)
A friend who always settles differences with reconciliation.	Jesus and Peter (Luke 22)
A friend who cheers when you find other friends.	Jesus' disciples (John 1:35–42)
A friend who loves expecting nothing in return.	Jesus and Judas (John 13)
A friend who is never jealous and does not compete with you.	Barnabas and Paul (Acts 4–15)
A friend who respects your boundaries.	Barnabas and Paul (Acts 15)
A friend who gives you a second chance.	Mark and Paul (Acts 15:36–39, 2 Timothy 4:11)
A friend who is committed to your development.	Aquila, Priscilla, and Apollos (Acts 18)
A friend who joins you in hardship.	Paul and Luke (Acts 27–28)

The Dish	The Servers
A friend who helps you get rid of things that keep you from God.	Paul and Peter (Galatians 2)
A friend who will be your partner.	Paul, Timothy, and Epaphroditus (Philippians 2)
A friend who makes you wiser.	Paul and Timothy (1 and 2 Timothy)
A friend who won't judge your past but challenges you for the future.	Paul and Onesimus (Philemon 1)

11

Love by Any Other Name Is Not the Same

The most popular Scripture recited at weddings is the passage known as the love chapter. In concise but poetic terms, 1 Corinthians 13 lays out the responsibilities of love. I didn't include the iconic reading in my own wedding, as I didn't want inconvenient truth to spoil my self-centered fantasy. I was operating under the belief that not only would the wedding be all about me, but the marriage would be too.

As I looked into my groom's eyes and he promised to love me, cherish me, honor me (are you hearing a theme there?), I heard affirmation that I was the center of the whole shebang. He swears that I also vowed to love, honor, and cherish him, but honestly, who can say. With no video, it is my word against his. Even if I did say it, at that moment, I was only dreaming about how wonderful life would be now that I had someone to focus on me until death stepped between us.

Fast-forward a mere three days to an outing on our honeymoon. Like any respectable princess living in her own dream, we went to Walt Disney World to celebrate the start of our lives together. I had planned all the magical places in the park we would visit. Then, just as I was reveling in my newfound significance, I heard my groom announce, "I don't care about you anymore."

In the interest of fairness, he swears all he said was, "Why don't we visit the Space Center today instead of Disney?" I knew what he meant. Marriage wasn't going to be all about me after all. It would start with a visit to the space shuttle, escalating until eventually I would be watching ESPN with him instead of the Hallmark Channel. Where would it stop?

It took several years to fully come to terms with the inconvenient truth that marriage is about *us*, not just about *me*. I hope it has not been equally shocking for you to discover that the same is true of the union of friends. It is as much an official *us* union as if we had stood before witnesses and exchanged friendship rings. That brings us back to 1 Corinthians 13. No better passage in all of Scripture describes the covenant responsibilities of *us* relationships in all their forms.

That is why the passage is far more than a marriage staple. It is a primer for how to express love in any mutual relationship. It is, Jesus reveals, the first responsibility of friendship and its main ingredient. It is how Jesus brought us into relationship with himself and made us His friends, through extreme, laying-aside-His-life kind of love that also points the way to our friendships with one another.

> This is my commandment, that you love one another as I have loved you. Greater love has no one than this, that someone lay down his life for his friends. You are my friends if you do what I command you. No longer do I call you servants, for the servant does not know what his master is doing; but I have called you friends, for all that I have heard from my Father I have made known to you. You did not choose me, but I chose you and appointed you that you should go and bear fruit and that your fruit should abide, so that whatever you ask the Father in my name, he may give it to you. These things I command you, so that you will love one another. (John 15:12–17 ESV)

Friendship is love. Love is friendship. The only way to create a true life-giving friendship patterned after the friend who loved us first is by loving. It is the glue that sticks *us* together through time, circumstances, and our flawed humanity. Without it, we have only varying degrees of commitment held together by self-interest.

That Loving Feeling

The love Jesus speaks of is not just a whole bunch of feelings. Don't misunderstand. I have deep affection for my friends. I am joyful when I am with them. They make me feel protective, proud, excited, and hopeful. Feelings, though, are fickle things affected by a myriad of circumstances from hormones to the effects of stress. I feel more affection toward everybody after 9 a.m. or with a bag of M&Ms in hand. Even though emotions are part of our image bearing (God has emotions), our emotions have been compromised by sin and self and too much caffeine. If they are the only basis for our love relationships (with friends, family, spouses), then we have built on shifting sand. When God talks about His love for us, He talks about more than emotions. His love is built on the solid rock of action.

- Because of His love, *He keeps his promises.* (Deuteronomy 7:9)
- *His love provides us a refuge.* (Psalm 36:7)
- *His love is merciful, gracious, slow to anger and abounding in faithfulness.* (Psalm 86:15)
- Through His love, *He gives a covenant of peace.* (Isaiah 54:10)
- He loved us with an everlasting love, therefore *He continued His faithfulness.* (Jeremiah 31:3)
- In His love, *He quiets us* and *sings over us.* (Zephaniah 3:17)
- For God so loved us *He gave His Son.* (John 3:16)

- Because He loves us, *He makes His home with us.* (John 14:23)
- Because of His love, *He has given us His own Spirit.* (Romans 5:5)
- God shows His love for us in that *Christ died for us.* (Romans 5:8)
- Because of His great love toward us, *He shows us mercy.* (Ephesians 2:4)
- Because of His great love for us, *He made us alive in Christ.* (Ephesians 2:4–5)
- In His love, *He saves* without regard to our efforts. (Titus 3:4–5)
- In His love for us, *He disciplines us.* (Hebrews 12:6)
- In His love, *He takes our anxieties* on himself. (1 Peter 5:6–7)
- See what kind of love God has for us that *God has adopted us.* (1 John 3:1)
- By His love, *He covers our sins.* (1 John 4:10)
- His love *drives out fear.* (1 John 4:18)

The list is much longer, but you can see the record is clear: God loves with action. He is love, but He also does love. The entire foundation of our relationship with Him is built on what He has done and is doing. God doesn't just feel a fondness because we are so wonderful and irresistible. Remember, we were His enemies when He reached out His hands of love to us on the cross (Romans 5:10). His actions were unmerited and based on His own loving character. Jesus said that our love should also be characterized by action:

> Anyone who loves me will *obey my teaching.* My Father will love them, and we will come to them and make our home with them. (John 14:23, emphasis added)

> This is love for God: to *keep his commands.* And his commands are not burdensome. (1 John 5:3, emphasis added)

Our first responsibility in our preeminent *us* relationship with our friend Jesus is to love with action: keep His commands. It is the only adequate response to His great act of friendship on the cross. Keeping His commands, Jesus said, "As I have done, go and do likewise." Those who love in the model of Christ's love will love others with action.

The Secret to Action-Packed Love

Chapter 13 of 1 Corinthians holds the secret to action-packed love. Koine Greek, the original language of the New Testament, consists of several words to convey the idea of love, while English has only one. I love pizza and I love my mother (not in that order, Mom). English doesn't have options to delineate kinds or degrees of love. Ours is a one-size-fits-all word. In the language of the New Testament, the variety of words helps us understand why this wonderful passage is applicable to the art of friendship.

If it were only instructing couples on how to practice romantic love, God would have selected the Greek word for romantic love, *eros*. It isn't defining just parental or familial love—that would be *storge*. It isn't exclusively instructing on love for our greater Christian community—that love would be *philia*. The love extolled in this iconic passage is specifically the highest of all forms of love, *agape*. Agape is divine love. It is the love that defines God's selfless, sacrificial, unconditional, unmerited love for us. It is the love the Father has for the Son (see John 15:9). It is demonstrative love that goes beyond emotion and moves God to extend all of those wonderful expressions of His benevolence that we enjoy. It is a love that keeps on loving even when it is not reciprocal. Agape is a love that focuses on the good of the other even at great cost. It is a love that delights to give.

To whom would teachings on agape apply? They apply to anyone who wants to love as God loves in any relationship. Friendship, being modeled on God's love, especially requires agape. Jesus was explicit in this:

> A new commandment I give you: [agapao] one another. As I have [agapao] you, so you must [agapao] one another. (John 13:34)

> Greater [agape] has no one than this: to lay down one's life for one's friends. (John 15:13)

Being joined as friends means embracing, adopting, and expressing God's agape love. So, "dearly beloved, we are gathered here today in the sight of God to join these friends in the bonds of holy friendship. . . ." Cue the reading of 1 Corinthians 13.

Being joined as friends means embracing, adopting, and expressing God's agape love.

As you read through what is essentially a guide to the art of friendship, you'll notice that I have inserted the original Greek word *agape*. Each time you see it, picture God's divine love in action. Let that image supersede all other associations you have of love. Picture instead how God's divine agape demonstrates friendship to you.

> If I speak in the tongues of men or of angels, but do not have [agape], I am only a resounding gong or a clanging cymbal. If I have the gift of prophecy and can fathom all mysteries and all knowledge, and if I have a faith that can move mountains, but do not have [agape], I am nothing. If I give all I possess to the poor and give over my body to hardship that I may boast, but do not have [agape], I gain nothing.
>
> [Agape] is patient, [agape] is kind. It does not envy, it does not boast, it is not proud. [Agape] does not dishonor others, it is not self-seeking, it is not easily angered, it keeps no record of wrongs. [Agape] does not delight in evil but rejoices with the truth. [Agape] always protects, always trusts, always hopes, always perseveres. [Agape] never fails. (1 Corinthians 13:1–8)

Aren't you glad God agapes you! Consider how powerful it is in your life that God is patient with you. That He is not easily angered, nor does He keep a record of your wrongs. We certainly give Him ample reasons to lose patience, or to scold us for our ever-growing list of offenses. Yet He is a friend who protects us. In response to what He actively does and what He actively withholds, our own commitment toward Him increases. That kind of love is powerful—and our friends need it from us.

For the next three chapters, we are going to look in-depth at 1 Corinthians 13 from a horizontal view, that is, how we express agape to our friends. We have two sections to cover. First, we will consider cautions about what will not bring us acceptance or true friendship. Then we will examine the very specific do's and don'ts that make friendships healthy and satisfying.

Friendship Credentials

When it comes to leaving a mark on the world, the love chapter offers another of those upside-down realities: Prestige does not equal significance. You may be the most persuasive expositor (speaking even with the tongues of angels), or a giant among intellects (even prophetic with all knowledge), or the most generous philanthropist (sacrificially giving it all to the poor), and still gain absolutely nothing of eternal consequence. Even if your prestige is in the form of spiritual gifting, absent the motive and expressions of agape toward other people, the effort to be something will come to a huge, disappointing zero.

Think how counterintuitive this is in our attempts to win friends. The norm is to approach friendship as if we are applying for a job. "If I can just impress you with my qualifications (spiritual or otherwise), will you choose me?" Surreptitiously, in our conversations with prospects, we let slip our achievements here and there, hoping to get noticed. We sprinkle in the people we know, places we've been, things we've accomplished, or ways we have God's blessings. We try not to be too obvious, but impressing others seems a logical pathway to building friendships. We lay our best selves out there with the silent plea, *Somebody, please, pick me!* It is a crazy emotional roller coaster. But worse than that, it is a vain exercise.

Instead of walking away with authentic friendships, we feel judged at worst and insecure at best. Either we work to meet or retain the expectation we set, or we worry that they care only about the prestige we promoted. *What will happen when they get to know the real me? Will they change their mind?* An approach to relationships based on our qualifications will eventually lead to instability because it is just more evidence that we are operating from the *It's all about me* viewpoint. Worse, we gain nothing. Neither does our friend.

Jesus had every reason to boast. If anyone had a path to winning friends because of personal prestige, it was the actual Son of God, but that wasn't His strategy. What He did was so radical that Paul would have to specifically call us out of the norm of elevating ourselves to follow His example:

> Have this mind among yourselves, which is yours in Christ Jesus, who, though he was in the form of God, did not count equality with God a thing to be grasped, but emptied himself, by taking the form of a servant, being born in the likeness of men. And being found in human form, he humbled himself by becoming obedient to the point of death, even death on a cross. (Philippians 2:5–8 ESV)

It is good to take inventory of all the Lord has provided in your life. The apostle Paul certainly did—and he had plenty to consider. In both his letter to the Philippians and his letter to the Corinthians, he had occasion to recount his résumé. And his conclusion after detailing his impressive credentials: We "who worship by the Spirit of God and glory in Christ Jesus, put no confidence in the flesh" (Philippians 3:3 ESV).

There is no shame in being humanly or spiritually persuasive, intellectual, or generous. Sure, they are honorable aspirations, but absent the surpassing value of love, they are useless. They are certainly not prerequisites for friendship. Nor are there special advantages in pursuing them. Apart from agape love, while our skills, talents, accolades, and gifts might be helpful on a résumé, they will not help you make or keep significant covenant friendships. I hope that is a relief to you. You can stop striving to be worthy and put down the mask. You, not your accomplishments, are the treasure you offer to friends. The love you offer far outweighs anything else you bring to the table. That reality certainly levels the playing field. There is no one too great or too lowly who cannot master the real art of friendship. You don't have to think of friending as a competition—unless you want to out-agape others. No one will complain about that!

You can stop striving to be worthy and put down the mask. You, not your accomplishments, are the treasure you offer to friends.

Reflect with God

Talk to God about what insights you have discovered about yourself and His calling to friendship. Thank Him that you are enough in His sight. Confess any *It's all about me* attitudes that have been part of your pursuit of friends. Thank Him for new understanding, and ask Him to help you cling to what is true as you seek to express sincere agape in friendships.

- When have you been impressed by someone's "credentials"? In what ways did you find yourself competing with their status? How did this impact your relationship?
- What have you done to get someone you wanted to impress to recognize you for your achievement, connection, or position?

- Have you been tempted to exaggerate your credentials to be liked? How did that approach make you feel about yourself?
- In what ways did this help or hurt your new relationship?
- How has the opening section of 1 Corinthians 13 helped reorient your thinking in regard to the process of pursuing friends?
- In what ways has it freed you from performance?

12

Love Is . . .

I love shortcuts. I buy my groceries no more than twenty items at a time just so I can use the express lane. I'm of the school of work-smarter-not-harder. Unfortunately, as Little Red Riding Hood learned, some shortcuts can lead to big delays. It takes maturity to know the difference between a legitimate time-saving alternative and a cop-out. This is a lesson I taught (and had to learn) many times in family life. One son in particular is as shortcut prone as his mom. Like God often does with me, I let him discover through experience the hazards that can bring.

The night before a sixth-grade spelling test, he was confident he had studied enough for the exam. When I suggested we go through our normal written drills, he declined.

"I don't need to do that," he assured me. "Writing them is a waste of time. Trust me, Mom. I've studied enough."

I had to wonder if this might be one of those teachable moments. He was convinced he had discovered a better way to prepare for success than generations of academics before him. Did I dare let him test that theory? I did, with a warning.

"If you make at least a 90 percent, you can skip the drills the rest of the year. But if your grade drops, we've got a problem."

While I was skeptical, I hoped this shortcut would be an overwhelming success. My life would be easier if I had less homework to oversee. It was not a success. When my son got home from school the next day, I inquired about the spelling test.

"Oh, that," he said. "I have a paper you need to sign."

With that, he returned to the formula that gives results—study, practice, study, practice, study, practice. As anticipated, his grades reflected the effort. I can't blame him for trying.

Though some shortcuts work, some aspects of life have no successful shortcuts. Making and keeping life-giving friendships are on that list.

Perhaps you have tried some of the common friending shortcuts. Have you tried flattery to win someone's affection rather than faithfulness? Do you spend more time "liking" on social media than liking people in person? Have you substituted someone's 140-character thoughts for finding out what is really on their heart? Does it seem faster and safer to get someone's interest by pretending to be something you're not instead of building trust? Has your busy life left you making quality time a substitute for investing the quantity of time your friends really need? Or maybe you are stuck in the shortcut of playing hard to get, waiting for them to come to you. These are the shortcuts we pin our hopes on to bring about A+ relationships with D– effort.

If that strategy hasn't worked for you, I have some great news. Study and practice can turn the results around. God wants you to succeed at creating and keeping meaningful friendships. He not only modeled it for us, but He spelled out the particulars so we can know and practice them. We have already seen that friendship is spelled l-o-v-e, or more specifically, a-g-a-p-e. The unique character of agape has a list of qualities that makes it distinct from any other kind of love. It is in expressing these qualities to others that relationships deepen and solidify. These qualities lived out are so compelling they make us a friend to whom others are attracted.

Of course, the irony is that these expressions of love don't focus on what they get in return. The double irony is that they can't help but bring a return, but only for those who have taken the time to understand and practice the true nature of agape. That means skipping the shortcuts and putting in the effort.

The Do's and Don'ts of Action-Packed Love

Fourteen words combine on our love list from the love chapter that together spell out *agape*. Some are words we must learn to practice (*love is*) and some are words we must learn not to practice (*love is not*).

Love is . . . patient, kind, truthful, protecting, trusting, hopeful, persevering.

Love is not . . . envious, boastful, prideful, dishonoring, selfish, angry, resentful.

Agape love is not complete until we learn and practice these words; that means friendship is not complete. While each word stands alone, each is also part of the whole in much the same way as the parts of the fruit of the Spirit manifest a whole. It isn't called *fruits* of the Spirit. It is one fruit that yields nine essential qualities in a full expression of the Spirit of God. It would not be an exaggeration to say that the fifteen qualities of agape are actually the fruit of love. Love, when given its full expression, will produce (or restrain) these specific qualities. Let's look at two pairs of qualities where the practice of the positive attribute eradicates the practice of the negative.

Love Is Patient; Love Is Not Easily Angered

They say you should never pray for patience because God will send circumstances that require you to practice patience. I don't believe that is true. Life is already one big opportunity to practice patience. We ought to be more concerned with why we are asking God to divinely bestow patience. Could it be we hope for a shortcut to spare us the effort required to practice what He has already made available? I am preaching to the choir here, sister. When people do what people do and act like people, I throw up the pleading prayer, "Lord, give me patience." In response, He usually brings to mind this conveniently forgotten truth: *I have already given you everything you need for godliness.*

The problem isn't that we don't have what it takes to treat others with patience, but that we don't use what we have. Yet nothing is more foundational to love than patience. To understand why, we have to understand what agape patience is and what it is not. It is not simply surrendering to circumstances we can't change. That is not patience; that is defeat. It is not having a *Who cares?* attitude; that is apathy. It is not denial, indulgence, or futility. Agape patience is the antithesis of those things.

Again, it is instructive to look at the original language in which these words were sovereignly recorded to gain the most accurate understanding of what God is spelling out for us. Patience, in this instance, is the Greek word *makrothymeo*. The New King James Version most accurately renders it "Love suffers long." It is certainly not the whole picture of love, but agape is willing, and should expect, to endure the pains of being in relationships with people. *Makrothymeo* is love that opts out of taking the escape clause when things get hard. Even more than just sticking with it, Thayer's Greek Lexicon unpacks it further: "to be patient in bearing the offences and injuries of others; to be mild and slow in avenging; to be long-suffering, slow to anger, slow to punish" and "to persevere patiently and bravely in enduring misfortunes and troubles."[1] *A Greek–English Lexicon of the New Testament (BDAG)* adds that to be long-suffering is "to bear up under provocation without complaint."[2]

How is that for spelling it out clearly? Agape bears offenses, provocations, and injuries while being mild and not vengeful, withholding anger and complaint. Lord, give me patience! We like to complain when we are offended. We desire revenge, even if it is just a snappy comeback. Being mild is what we call boring. Yet expressed as God expresses it, this love is incredibly dynamic. Peter explained,

> The Lord is not slow to fulfill his promise as some count slowness, but is patient toward you, not wishing that any should perish, but that all should reach repentance. (2 Peter 3:9 ESV)

God expresses *makrothymeo* not from a place of weakness or as a victim, but in power to bring about an eternal purpose: reconciliation with those who are separated from Him. That is the potential of patience. God makes an invitation of friendship to those who provoke and offend Him. Through His long-suffering nature, He does not rescind the offer, but bears the insults, provocations, and injuries without anger or retribution. Agape love waits. It is not in a hurry to get an outcome. It leaves the door open so that rather than love lost, love can be gained and relationships can be reconciled. It will take an act of God for us to offer this kind of patient love to our friends, because it is not natural.

Where this kind of patience prevails, anger is ruled out. *Agape is not easily angered*. The word is *paroxyno*, and Thayer expands its meaning to include being irritated, provoked, exasperated, or spurred on to anger.[3] It is the very opposite of waiting. Rather than making room at provoking times, anger slams the door shut (probably after coming back into the room a time or two to express outrage like a hormonal teen). The volatility of anger will quickly stifle the hope of reconciliation that is patience's purpose. One outburst can bring consequences that are hard to undo.

Moses, a man God spoke to as "one speaks to a friend" (Exodus 33:11), had faithfully led the complaining, disgruntled Israelites through the desert for thirty-eight years until they were nearing the time of God's promise to enter into the land of Canaan. The people were his brothers and sisters, his countrymen, and his friends. These were fellow heirs of God's promises. Yet again, fearful circumstances caused them to freak out. They had no water in the wilderness of Zin, where God had led them. So they started arguing and complaining.

> The people quarreled with Moses and said, "Would that we had perished when our brothers perished before the LORD! Why have you brought the assembly of the LORD into this wilderness, that we should die here, both we and our cattle? And why have you made us come up out of Egypt to bring us to this evil place? It is no place for grain or figs or vines or pomegranates, and there is no water to drink." (Numbers 20:3–5 ESV)

Moses' first response was to fall on his face before God to intercede for the needs of his people. God honored his prayers and told Moses to speak to the rock in their midst, and God would bring forth water and satisfy the people. Moses did go out, but he was not happy. Provoked by their ingratitude, complaining, and lack of faith, he did more than God commanded.

> Moses and Aaron gathered the assembly together before the rock, and he said to them, "Hear now, you rebels: shall we bring water for you out of this rock?" And Moses lifted up his hand and struck the rock with his staff twice, and water came out abundantly, and the congregation drank, and their livestock. (Numbers 20:10–11 ESV)

Moses let himself be provoked into responding with anger, displayed by striking the rock and giving them an earful. Whether they deserved his anger really isn't the point, at least not to God. Moses' angry display threw a monkey wrench in the greater things God desired to accomplish.

> The LORD said to Moses and Aaron, "Because you did not believe in me, to uphold me as holy in the eyes of the people of Israel, therefore you shall not bring this assembly into the land that I have given them." These are the waters of Meribah, where the people of Israel quarreled with the LORD, and through them he showed himself holy. (Numbers 20:12–13 ESV)

Impatience seems to expose two things. First, that we don't believe God. Second, that we care more about offenses to us than we care about the glory of God. God had a purpose in His patient provision of water. He wanted to show His glory, which He knew would be magnified in light of their ungrateful complaining. Moses, as a representative for God, distorted His glory with his outburst. He did not believe God that patience was the path to blessing. In the end, impulsive anger cost everyone. God forbade Moses from entering the Promised Land, the people were given a distorted view of God's mercy, and God was robbed of His glory.

When we are impatient, easily provoked, and moved to anger, we are guilty of the same unbelief. Do we not believe that God sees the offenses? Are we unwilling to trust that He can use the contrast between our agape patience and the affronts of others to reveal His glory and bring about good purposes? Love is patient, withholding reprisal, because patience leaves a door open for reconciliation and a more accurate display of God's glory as the friend who suffers long.

Boundaries in friendships are important. Occasionally, the Lord will lead us to step back. Even in those circumstances, when offenses require a response, agape will always lead with a longsuffering posture that is not easily provoked, petty, or vengeful.

Thinking back to David and his friendship not with Jonathan but with Saul, we see this lived out. Time and time again, both in word and deed, Saul caused David suffering. David eventually had to put distance between them, but patience was the guard he set around his heart so those offenses did not cause bitterness. His willingness to suffer long and not retaliate, even when given the chance, left him with hope. Perhaps God would move and their relationship would be restored. David refused to close the door to God's work and purposes in his life or Saul's just to attain short-term satisfaction. Patient love was an expression of and a catalyst for his hope, while the outcome was in God's hands.

You already know that Saul chose not to walk through that open door. And not everyone will. That doesn't mean all is lost.

In fact, much is gained. The very process of loving with a long-suffering nature makes us more like the Friend we long to imitate. "Not only so, but we also glory in our sufferings, because we know that suffering produces perseverance; perseverance, character; and character, hope" (Romans 5:3–4).

Consider your past and present friendships. What provokes you? How has anger closed doors? How would practicing agape patience have impacted the outcome or your maturity? What specific circumstances now give you the opportunity for agape patience?

Confess to the Lord where you have suffered short and closed doors. Ask Him to stir your heart each time someone inconveniences or offends you so you see your choice to put His glory and reputation above your own. As you practice this agape love, watch for the response in those who receive friendship that is patient and not easily angered. Watch what it does in your own heart.

Love Is Kind; Love Is Not Dishonoring

Where patience is love that holds back, kindness is love that presses in. It is the active complement to patience. To be kind, *chrēsteúomai*, is to act in ways that are "loving and merciful."[4] Thayer said it is "to use kindness."[5] It is not being nice. It is not a kindly feeling. It is a demonstration of loving mercy. Consider the model.

> At one time we too were foolish, disobedient, deceived and enslaved by all kinds of passions and pleasures. We lived in malice and envy, being hated and hating one another. But when the kindness and love of God our Savior appeared, he saved us, not because of righteous things we had done, but because of his mercy. He saved us through the washing of rebirth and renewal by the Holy Spirit. (Titus 3:3–5)

Kindness is friendship offered where there is need without regard to another's capacity to repay the kindness. God knew all too well that what we carried (our sin) was a burden too heavy for us to bear. His kindness took action to meet our need by bringing salvation. That is friendship. It is so important to God that we imitate Him in this, that He would rather we express merciful kindness than offer rituals and sacrifices. In God's own words,

> He has told you, O man, what is good; and what does the LORD require of you but to do justice, and to love kindness, and to walk humbly with your God? (Micah 6:8 ESV)

Our culture likes to tout the power of random acts of kindness, but to be kind like God is anything but random. It's intentional. It understands the burdens of others and finds practical ways to carry some of the load. It is action that conveys hope and rescue. It is sacrificial and sometimes costly. It never looks for a return on investment. Agape kindness has no quid pro quo. It is a kindness that so fully trusts God to meet personal needs that it can turn outward to help meet the needs of others.

The book of Ruth is a beautiful example of agape kindness. It is an unfolding tale of people seeing the need in others and laying aside their own lives to meet it. It starts with a widow named Naomi who is heartbroken at not only the loss of her husband, but also her grown sons while they are living in a foreign land. When Naomi decides to leave Moab and return to her homeland of Israel, she shows kindness to her daughters-in-law by not claiming her right to keep them with her. They are young enough to remarry and start families, so in kindness that puts their needs above her own, she urges them to leave her. One of them, Ruth, refuses. She recognizes the heavy burden of grief on Naomi and lays aside her own life and marriage prospects to remain and carry the burden with her mother-in-law. She tells her, "Where you go I will go. . . .

Our culture likes to tout the power of random acts of kindness, but to be kind like God is anything but random.

Your people shall be my people, and your God shall be my God (Ruth 1:16 ESV).

The rest of the book is one example after another of intentional kindness. Ruth provides for Naomi. Boaz, a kinsman, provides for Ruth. Naomi looks after Ruth's future. Ruth and Boaz restore family to Naomi. It is a story that begins in sorrow and brokenness but is redeemed through intentional loving-kindness offered with no expectation of return. Not only is each of their individual stories redeemed, but God also uses this family in the line of Messiah.

God gave me the opportunity to practice intentional kindness in a relationship that took me to places I had no idea I would go. Our kids went to a small Christian school during their elementary years, and one of the blessings was the chance to get to know the other parents. One of those parents would change my life.

Terri was the single working mom of two boys, one in our older son's grade and one in our younger son's. I met her when our oldest kids were in fourth grade and Terri was battling cancer. She had few social connections, sparse community support, and not much of a safety net. I had no idea what I might have to offer to Terri, but at a Moms and Muffins breakfast at the school one morning, I introduced myself.

I had no plan. I just thought that maybe I could be an encouragement. That one small act of kindness began a lifelong meaningful friendship. Terri was only five feet tall, but she was a fierce woman who was determined to turn her battle against cancer into a daily victory of faith. It was clear that she needed friends to help her in that battle. I had friends to share. Soon, she was going to our church to meet some of them—and they became her friends too.

I couldn't cure her cancer, and I couldn't take away the physical suffering. But I could help her with her kids. I could listen to her fears. I could stand by her hospital bed. I could hang out and be a girlfriend. I did all those things. As did many other women who grew to love Terri and her boys. Before long, my husband was standing in as a father figure and also taking care of honey-do's at both our houses. Her boys spent as much time under our roof as ours spent under hers. They loved Terri, and we loved her sons. We were growing to be family to one another.

It was hard not to love Terri. She was hopeful, full of faith, a prayer warrior, and fun to be around. Her great gift to all her friends was to show us what it meant to walk with Jesus moment by moment. She was petite, but her faith was giant. My faith grew as a result. In time, her needs were also giant. Her cancer spread. Her fight was long. Her boys had moved into those rocky teen years while she was losing her battle. After nine wonderful, painful, memorable years, Terri asked one more act of kindness of us. Would we take care of her boys after she went to be with her heavenly Father?

Terri slipped away on a November night, and a new son slipped into our family to stay. While her younger son chose to go to other relatives, for twelve years and counting, Michael has become as much a son to us as our other boys. He is now married and the father of precious twin girls—Terri's granddaughters *and* mine. The legacy of a friendship that started from a small but intentional act of kindness over muffins has changed our family and hers.

- What impact might your intentional, sacrificial, no-strings-attached kindness have in the lives of others?
- Do you carry any resentment because a kindness was not returned?
- When you consider that God desires our kindness toward others more than our rituals, what in your attitude needs to change?
- How might turning the focus to the burdens of others and their needs change your perspective about your own situation?
- Who are three people you know right now who are carrying a heavy burden?
- What agape kindness would help lighten their load?

As kindness is used as an expression of love toward friends, it will not leave room for its nemesis, dishonor. "Love is not dishonoring." Your Bible may read that love is not rude, unseemly, or improper. From the Greek *aschēmoneō*, it translates, "does not act unbecomingly."[6] It is a complete absence of rudeness.

This has become a foreign concept today. Our culture has made trolling others on the internet a thing. It glorifies one-liners, elevates dysfunctional families to reality television, and rewards dirt-slinging politicians. We are a society that traffics in rudeness. If we're honest, we would have to admit that disrespect has infiltrated our hearts as well. Even in relationships we value, rudeness can creep in. Whether it is the overt rudeness of snarky sarcasm or the covert dishonor of telling it like it is, absent an aggressive posture of kindness, we can be sure the inertia of our culture and our own sinful nature will have us behaving in ways that devalue others. That is really the heart of *aschēmoneō*.

I don't have many precious objects in my house because the Wiers are not careful people. Between the menagerie of animals and the hustle of four kids, it would be an act of insanity to have valuable things. Too much happens too fast. The result is that we've never bothered guarding our belongings. Feet and dogs lived on couches. Kids played Nerf ball in the house. Even the pig made himself comfortable on the area rug. There is only one thing I value enough to zealously protect—my grandmother's glass candy dish. It is a green blown-glass bowl with a delicate bird alighting on the rim. It sat on my grandmother's coffee table for as far back as I can remember. When she passed away, that was my inheritance. It was the treasure I most wanted. I knew bringing it into our house would be a risk. It couldn't sit out just anyplace, so I put it inside the only secure location I had: a dish cabinet in the dining room. From the day it went on display, none of the kids were allowed to open the cabinet. If we needed dishes for guests, I got them myself rather than risk anything happening to my treasure. Many years of rowdy family life have passed, and many items have been broken or worn out, but my grandma's treasure is still safe because I actively guarded it from harm.

Not dishonoring is not simply biting your tongue or curbing your sarcasm. It isn't using good Southern manners. It is so valuing the other person that you go to great measures to protect them from damage by your own hands. That brings us back to kindness. Agape kindness is the protection, the safe place against rudeness and dishonor. We cannot be rude if we are intentionally seeking ways to act kindly. We will not dishonor if we value a person enough to set our own life aside to carry their burdens. Just as patience negates anger, so kindness disarms dishonor.

Appraising Your Attitude

- How have you taken your friends for granted, failing to value them as a treasure inherited from your Father?
- What habit have you developed that is actually a form of rudeness?
- What might you communicate to a friend by these habits?
- Where has the disrespectful nature of our culture impacted your thinking and given you license to dishonor?

Kindness protects every confidence shared with you, refuses to talk unfavorably about a friend to any other person, opts out of gossip at every opportunity, believes the best even after an offense, treats others with courtesy in every situation, gives preference to people over a cell phone when together, and listens with your full attention. Where patience and kindness excel, no room is left for anger and rudeness. Where anger and rudeness are given liberty, kindness and patience can never be served.

13

How to Lose a Friend in Ten Days

I am a big fan of romantic comedies. If I am going to pay money for a night at the movies, I want to feel good when I leave. Life has enough drama; I certainly don't need to pay for more. A movie that scores big for many rom-com fans is the classic *How to Lose a Guy in 10 Days*. At the heart of the story is a magazine writer's quest to prove that every woman will ruin a romantic relationship if she makes certain classic dating mistakes. To prove her point, and hopefully help her readers avoid that fate, Andie, played by Kate Hudson, randomly chooses a guy and sets about the task of driving him away in less than two weeks with a straightforward strategy: doing everything girls do wrong in relationships. "Basically, everything we know guys hate. I'll be clingy, needy—"

"Touchy-feely," her friend chimes in. "Oh, call him in the middle of the night and tell him everything you had to eat that day."

Only the third friend is clueless as to why these are mistakes, asking, "What's wrong with that?"

Thus the hilarious experiment begins. Andie catches a guy's attention being her real and charming self, and then flips the switch just when he is getting to know her. Sure enough, those bad relationship habits prove too much. He wants out fast, thus demonstrating that no emotionally healthy guy will stick with a clingy, needy girlfriend.

May I propose that the same is true of our friend relationships? Classic mistakes we make can lead to losing a friend just as quickly. And the plot twist is that we may be clueless to the mistakes we are making.

The remainder of the love chapter lists six classic mistakes that are almost always relationship killers. If 1 Corinthians 13 were a script about how to lose a friend in ten days, our character would say, "I'm gonna limit myself to doing everything girls would hate in a relationship. I'll be envious, proud, self-seeking, boastful, I'll hold a grudge, and I will secretly gloat when she gets what she deserves."

That is a classic strategy for getting dumped. No emotionally healthy person is looking for a friend like that. No spiritually healthy person will be a friend like that. So let's conduct a little experiment of our own. Look at each of the classic mistakes that break up friendships and see if any of them have crept into your relationships.

How to Lose a Friend—Be Envious

"Agape . . . is not envious."

From the Greek *zēloō*—to envy or be jealous.

If you are a Kate Hudson fan, then you have probably also seen her movie *Bride Wars*. It tells a story of two lifelong friends who have to come to terms with suppressed jealousies that surface under the pressure of wedding planning. It is a cautionary tale of the danger of unresolved jealousy and competition between friends. It's unlikely that making this classic mistake will lead to you being tackled by your best friend as you walk down the aisle, as Kate's character was, but it can clobber you in other ways.

The book of James, using the same Greek word, warns that it could actually lead to worse: "You lust and do not have; so you commit murder. You are envious (*zēloō*) and cannot obtain; so you fight and quarrel. You do not have because you do not ask" (James 4:2 NASB).

A sure sign that you are making the mistake of jealousy is that fighting and quarrelling will characterize your friendship. I wish I could give you a list of all the potential jealousy traps, but they are innumerable. Jealousy can happen over anything, big or small, material or personal. Any time we are discontent with our lot, there is fertile ground for envy. Do any of these seem familiar?

- When a friend tells you about an achievement, you mentally or verbally diminish the significance.
- You find yourself preoccupied with your friend's status or title, positively or negatively.
- You think about the unfairness of your friend's blessings.
- You feel competitive, wanting to outdo your friend with a better husband, kids, talent, spiritual growth, popularity, income, professional advancement, or material possessions.
- Your initial response to their good news is negative, feeling disappointment before you feel joy.
- You feel the need to prove that you had important or confidential news before she did, increasing your own feelings of self-importance.
- You hesitate in actively encouraging the success or affirmation of your friend.

All of these unfriendly (and unloving) attitudes, in reality, are not even about the friend. When they happen, they are about us. Whenever we are discontent with our own circumstances, someone else's provision magnifies the pain of our perceived (or real) poverty and stirs longings. Unable to get what we want, our defense is to diminish what they have. *My marriage is disappointing, so she doesn't deserve her mature husband because she is no better than me. I feel unseen and unappreciated, so any praise she receives for her accomplishment couldn't possibly be justified. I am not satisfied with my home, my clothes, or my car, so it is unfair that she gets so many more material blessings.*

Only our heart may say it or our mouths betray it. Either way, discontentment grows because we don't trust God to give us good things in His time. We may also be ungrateful for the good He has already given because we are preoccupied with comparing it. Envy is such a joy stealer that it cannot bear to see God's blessings in our friend's life. The result is a friendship weakened by jealousy. Getting more or being more won't resolve envy issues. Trusting more is the only remedy. The psalmist showed how to guard our hearts:

> Teach me your decrees, O Lord; I will keep them to the end. Give me understanding and I will obey your instructions; I will put them into practice with all my heart. Make me walk along the path of your commands, for that is where my happiness is found. Give me an eagerness for your laws rather than a love for money! Turn my eyes from worthless things, and give me life through your word. Reassure me of your promise, made to those who fear you. Help me abandon my shameful ways; for your regulations are good. I long to obey your commandments! Renew my life with your goodness. (Psalm 119:33–40 NLT)

How to Lose a Friend—Be Boastful, Be Proud

> "Agape does not boast and is not proud."

From the Greek *perpereuomai*—to act as a braggart, to show off as one who needs attention. From the Greek *phusioo*—to inflate, to puff up, to bear oneself lofty, arrogant.

When our kids were young, they loved to ride on their daddy's shoulders. To go from three feet tall to riding heads above everyone else was exhilarating. They delighted to lord their elevated stature over their siblings. The problem, of course, is that what goes up must come down. It didn't take them long to realize that those they taunted when they felt unreachable, they would encounter eye to eye when Daddy got tired of carrying them around. Then would come consequences.

That pretty well describes our situation when we let ourselves get lifted up by pride and carried away with boasting. Whatever the catalyst for that kind of self-indulgence, there are always consequences. We can count on it, because God himself is committed to bringing the proud down off their high horse: "God opposes the proud but shows favor to the humble" (James 4:6).

James was just echoing Jesus, who said, "Whoever exalts himself will be humbled, and whoever humbles himself will be exalted" (Matthew 23:12 ESV). Then Jesus immediately launched into a harsh denunciation of the most arrogant offenders of the day, the religious elites:

> Woe to you, teachers of the law and Pharisees, you hypocrites! You clean the outside of the cup and dish, but inside they are full of greed and self-indulgence. (Matthew 23:25)

And there we have the fruits of pride—greed and self-indulgence. It is what motivated Satan and brought about his banishment from heaven. He was greedy for the glory that was God's alone, and self-indulgent enough to think he deserved it: "You [Satan] said in your heart: 'I will ascend to the heavens; I will raise my throne above the stars of God. I will sit on the mount of assembly, on the utmost heights of Mount Zaphon. I will ascend above the tops of the clouds; I will make myself like the Most High'" (Isaiah 14:13–14).

By God's grace, I hope we are no longer competing for superiority with God. That is settled by those who confess Jesus as Lord.

Yet unless we fully appreciate the incredible value we are to God, proved by His agape love at the cross, we will still be greedy for approval from others. That greed, when indulged, gives rise to pride. Then boasting takes a piggyback ride on pride's shoulders to gain the attention it craves. That kind of elevation is so exhilarating we don't realize that it always comes at a cost. Consider the price the Bible describes:

> Pride goes before destruction, a haughty spirit before a fall. (Proverbs 16:18)
>
> Pride brings a person low. (Proverbs 29:23)

It will bring us and our relationships low because its approval-seeking nature makes us strive for lower things. If I prize a friend's recognition, I will begin to mold myself into the image of what I think my friend values most. I will try to be like them, only better. And whether that pursuit is of something earthly and vain, or good, noble, and right, pride distorts and undercuts the very accomplishment for which we strive. C. S. Lewis spoke to this dynamic.

> Pride gets no pleasure out of having something, only out of having more of it than the next man. . . . It is the comparison that makes you proud: the pleasure of being above the rest. Once the element of competition is gone, pride is gone.[1]

To strive for the pleasure of God is a humble exercise of dependence focused on bringing Him pleasure. To strive for the approval of people, even a friend, is an exercise in comparison and competition. In a way, that makes pride the equally worthless cousin of envy. Where envy wants and resents what others have, pride exalts in having what others might want. Both are products of insecurity. Both make us self-conscious and fearful of falling from the high place we have climbed to show ourselves worthy. That is why when challenged, the prideful person becomes defensive and argumentative. They are willing to sacrifice relationship and authenticity rather than risk exposure of weakness, aka unworthiness. Pride is desperate to keep its place on top. It will even resort to demeaning tactics to deflect criticism. All becomes fair to preserve the narrative that we are worth admiring. Pride, then, is given free reign so it can keep feeding the greedy craving for approval, but it will never be enough. No approval will ever fill the hunger of a person who chooses to pursue the approval of the world because they fail to know their value before God their Creator.

> Don't you know that friendship with the world means enmity against God? Therefore, anyone who chooses to be a friend of the world becomes an enemy of God. Or do you think Scripture says without reason that he jealously longs for the spirit he has caused to dwell in us? But he gives us more grace. That is why Scripture says: "God opposes the proud but shows favor to the humble." Submit yourselves, then, to God. Resist the devil, and he will flee from you. Come near to God and he will come near to you. . . . Humble yourselves before the Lord, and he will lift you up. (James 4:4–10)

It is not difficult to see how pride and boasting damage friendships. By their very nature, they undermine agape's self-sacrificial nature. We don't have to keep trying to get to the top. God will lift those with a humble heart.

How to Lose a Friend—Be Self-Seeking

> "Agape does not seek its own."

From the Greek *zéteó* and *heautou*—seeks the things of self.

Perhaps no classic relationship mistake is more at odds with sacrificial agape love than being self-seeking. It is the me-first attitude that says agape is for chumps. For the immature friend, self-sacrifice always has a limit. It doesn't mind looking out for the interests of others, unless it means it can't also look out for its own.

I'm not a super sports fan. Prior to having children, I veered a wide berth around sports fields. Raising kids, however, has taught me not only something about sports but a lot about life. As the thrill of victory and the agony of defeat played out on the various fields, they also offered lessons for winning at what really matters. Our oldest son was eleven when one of those lessons became part of the game.

We were on vacation during youth baseball tryouts, so our son missed the coaches' draft. An athletic kid, he was used to being a top pick in sports his previous seven years of baseball. This year, however, he was assigned to a team with twelve other boys who also missed the draft. As fate would have it, none of them had ever played baseball. Though each boy individually had some potential, together they played like the Keystone Cops. They had no idea how to work as a team, and by the ninth inning each week, they were all frustrated and barely speaking to each other. Needless to say, they couldn't win a game. Getting our son to suit up and head onto the field every week required a rousing pep talk.

You cannot win at relationships if you are constantly looking for the angle that puts your interests ahead of your friends.

"Mom, our team will never win. Please let me quit. It's embarrassing."

He was right—they probably would not win a game. But he was still part of a team.

"Honey," I encouraged, "you might not win, but you can help the team be better. Besides, you're building character. Just do the best you can and if the team doesn't win, you can still improve your own skills. Only fifteen more games to go. You can do it!"

The team didn't get better. We didn't let him quit. I don't think he built character because he complained constantly. They ended the season with zero wins and eighteen losses.

When circumstances or relationships become challenging, there is always a temptation to look out for number one. Friendship, however, is a team sport. You cannot win at relationships if you are constantly looking for the angle that puts your interests ahead of your friends. You might win, but friendships lose.

A self-seeker isn't always obvious at first. A selfish person who sees a need that friends can fill in her life will initially behave in a way to attract them. She might begin a relationship helpfully, concerned, and others-focused because she is actually putting herself first in her desire to have friends. Perhaps she willingly mentors you, but rather than doing so for your sake, it is because it makes her feel important. Maybe she includes you in social circles because she knows you will build her up in front of others. She could be generous, but only because she needs the affirmation of your gratitude to feel significant. At some point, her "me first" motives will rise to the surface, and her friends will begin to feel used. Perhaps you have had a "me first" friend and recognize moves from her self-centered playbook:

- She won't compromise to make room for your preferences or ideas.
- She expends a lot of energy persuading you to her point of view.
- She is often late, cancels plans, or fails to follow up as expected.
- She doesn't return your calls or texts quickly, but expects that you will.
- She doesn't normally have time to hear your problems, but expects your undivided attention.
- She often redirects the conversation to her own issues.
- She rarely asks questions about you, but can talk about herself at length.
- She is possessive of your friendship but does not include you with her other friends.
- She uses charm and flattery to deflect negative attention and keep your friendship.
- She has a difficult time with boundaries.

- She often seeks to be the center of attention.
- She claims a very busy schedule when you are in need of help.

Read the list again, only this time substitute *I* in place of *She*. Do any of the self-seeking habits describe you? Agape calls us to sacrificial friendship, the polar opposite of friendship that seeks the things of self. One way to test your level of me-firstism is to ask yourself why you were aggravated the last time you had a little drama with a friend. If the answer is because she inconvenienced *you*, disappointed *you*, or kept *you* from getting what *you* wanted, then *you* might be the problem. Were you expecting all the sacrifices and compromises to be on her part? Did you lose all contentment because you did it her way? Those feelings can be a red flag that you have lost sight of what agape friendship is: *sacrificial* love that lays down its own way for a friend. A self-seeker will always prefer to take the ball and go home rather than suffer any kind of loss to be a friend.

When our son found working with others too costly, he took up tennis. At first, he enjoyed the independence and loved excelling with no one to hold him back. As time went on, he confessed that he missed the camaraderie of teammates. Eventually, he decided the price of getting what he wanted alone was costlier than sometimes losing with teammates. Ironically, the next team he joined was basketball, a sport for which my child had little aptitude. I started polishing my "there will be other seasons" speech, just in case. It turns out I didn't need it.

From the first game it was evident there was something special about this team. It wasn't the impressive stature of the kids: some were very short, others were tall, some were skinny, and others stout. They came from different schools and ethnic backgrounds, and none was a basketball prodigy. They were an unremarkable group—until they worked together. They anticipated one another's moves. They depended on one another's strengths, knew one another's weaknesses, and always stuck together. If one fouled out, another was there to spur him on. High-fives were always flying, and no one ever jeered a blown play or a bad shot. The longer they were together, the better the team became. They liked one another, gave their personal best to the team, and listened to the coach. There was no star player, but rather a group who helped one another be the best they could be. They were a dream team no one expected. The payoff was an incredible undefeated season that taught us all that winning is found when we spend the best of ourselves on someone other than ourselves. If you don't want to be part of a team like that, expect to lose friends.

How to Lose a Friend—Hold a Grudge

"Agape does not take into account wrong suffered."

From the Greek *logizomai* and *kakos*—does not calculate, add up, or take into account wrong thinking, feeling, or acting.

My brain houses a filing system that seems to have a default setting to record and easily retrieve a full list of hurts, snubs, offenses, grievances, insults, rejections, and wrongs, real or perceived. In this file are all the emotions that accompany the injuries I suffered. It is a huge file. I'm sure you have one too.

We can't have friends without having a few wounds. Even the most mature friendships involve offenses. It's inevitable because all of our friends miss the mark of perfection. Certainly, we know we miss the mark. It is both naïve and unrealistic, then, to assume that just because we love, we won't also hurt each other.

Like almost everything else we have discovered about friendship mistakes, grudges too are really more about our weaknesses than our friends. Grudges allow us to occupy the high moral ground as a person who has been wronged. As we add up the record of offenses, we get to be the sufferer in our own drama. Rehearse the offenses enough and we have a new identity: victim. Victimhood is the closest thing to martyrdom most of us will get. It puts us in a place to receive compassion, empathy, and affirmation. It gives us control over those who have wronged us, ammunition for retaliation, and justification for our lack of forgiveness. But counting our friends' sins against them also undermines trust, feeds self-centeredness, and mocks the foundational act of God's friendship. This is our example:

> God was reconciling the world to himself in Christ, not counting people's sins against them. And he has committed to us the message of reconciliation. (2 Corinthians 5:19)

Agape closes the file that holds the record of wrongs, not in denial that they ever happened, but rather leaves them unaccessed. As providence would have it, as I sat typing these very words, my computer glitched and shut down the document. When I reopened the program, the last *one thousand words* had not been saved. They were gone. I stared unbelieving at the screen. It was as if they had never even been written. My mind was a complete blank. I couldn't remember a single sentence to try to reconstruct what I had just completed. I stared, muttering, "No, no, no, no." I closed the program and opened it again, but not one single missing letter reappeared. I went through every technical gyration I knew but could not find the last version. Yet I knew that my computer did regular autosaves in the background. Where was the file?

After a desperate Google search, I found four suggested methods to retrieve autosaved documents after a crash. The first three produced nothing. The fourth required going in the back door of the developer files. I followed the instructions carefully, copying and pasting code the article provided to get into files I didn't even know existed. Jackpot! I found a folder named "Temporary," and in it, one file named "AutoRecoverySave." When I opened it, every word I had written was there. As I reread the pages, it was all familiar again. I remembered writing every word. What's amazing is that until I got hold of the file, I couldn't remember even one word.

Want to know how to lose a friend quickly? Go digging around in the files where past hurts and offenses are stored. Each time you retrieve an offense, remembering it, dwelling on it, or arming yourself with it, you let it write the hurts all over again. No new story can be written when you are too busy recounting past hurts. That is not love, even of self, because no one wins in that scenario.

Agape has the capacity to absorb offenses. It doesn't pretend they did not happen. It counts them; it just doesn't count them against the other. It bears the burden of filing them away rather than flinging them in revenge. Agape calculates that the relationship matters more than the offense. Of course, some damaging offenses do require boundaries, or even others who can help examine the file and help us wisely move forward. A relationship may even need to be set aside. Those are rare. We are not talking about those exceptional circumstances. The barbs and wounds of friends that are bound to happen in relationships with other imperfect people are the files to keep closed. There we depend on grace to share life with maturing friends who have their flaws as we have ours.

How do we do that? We die, just like Jesus. Jesus died to himself before He died on the cross. He died to His legitimate right to impose justice for those who offended Him as a holy God—that's us. To release others from their much smaller debt to us, we also have to die to self. We have to surrender the right to be right, to be recompensed, to be vindicated, and to be a victim. Then, and only then, can we lay down our lives with forgiveness. Only then can we resist the urge to dig into the files and reread the past.

Praise God, we won't always carry that folder full of hurts. Like my buried computer file, the folders that hold our wounds are labeled "Temporary." God has promised the day will come when He will make all things new. He will wipe away every tear and the offenses that caused them, both the offenses done to us and those done by us. Why, then, would we dig into files that God himself is determined to delete? Agape will always choose to keep the file closed, friending as if the offense never even happened.

How to Lose a Friend—Gloat Over Sin

"Agape does not rejoice in wrongdoing."

From the Greek *chairō* and *adikia*—to cheer about unrighteousness of heart and life.

The first sports experience for our son was not baseball or basketball. It was on a peewee soccer team for four-year-olds. Soccer is a great sport for moms because the littles are exhausted when they come home. The whole thing amounts to chasing a ball in mass, first one way and then the other. Most of the time Chase had no idea why he was running; he was just following the crowd. But as they say, even a blind squirrel finds an acorn sometimes. In a moment of blind luck and some confusion, our little guy got his foot on the ball and kicked it right into the goal. His teammates rejoiced with abandon. Even the other team cheered wildly. Our coach just put his head in his hands. Our little guy had scored a goal for the other team.

The prophet Isaiah warned that a time would come when people would cheer for the wrong team: "Woe to those who call evil good, and good evil; who substitute darkness for light and light for darkness; who substitute bitter for sweet and sweet for bitter!" (Isaiah 5:20 NASB).

We are living in that time. What once was universally rejected as ungodly behavior is now universally accepted by the culture. Good is called evil and evil is called good, but God's standards have not changed. Jesus calls His friends to follow His example and hate what is evil, not cheer for it. When we celebrate "wrongdoing," we put not only ourselves at risk, but also our friends, whom we often take along.

- Have you cheered gossip by spreading it to others?
- Do you lack moderation?
- Do you root for friends when they complain?
- Do you celebrate unworthy movies, books, or television shows?

- Have new cultural standards softened your commitment to biblical standards?
- Do you justify your sin or theirs in the name of friendship?
- Do you withhold the whole truth from a friend who is in obvious wrongdoing?

Noted pastor and theologian John MacArthur said, "Love never takes satisfaction from sin, whether it be our own or the sins of others."[2] Love will never make wrong appear right. It is always easier to run in the wrong direction when you find a group who will cheer your choices, and it is easier to cheer a friend than to tell her she just ran the wrong way. The essence of biblical life-sharing friendship is running together toward God and running together away from what is evil.

Agape friendship does not stop at our own rejection of sin. It also disallows our satisfaction when others are caught in sin. The French writer La Rochefoucauld noted that "the tribulations of our best friends arouse a sentiment in us that is not entirely unpleasant."[3] If we have let the other classic mistakes become part of our relationships, we can be sure that unbridled self will do some secret rejoicing when our friends suffer a fall.

We do it all the time when opposition political leaders have a scandal, a sacrilegious celebrity has a crisis, or someone we don't like gets caught in wrongdoing. We are well-practiced at not loving our enemies because it validates our feelings that they deserve their circumstances. I will be the first to admit that when a breaking news story reports the ruin of someone who I know stands against God's principles, a voice in my head says, *Well, they got what they deserved.* Until a voice in my heart says, *I spared you what you deserved.*

Agape whispers the same to us when we are tempted to secretly cheer when circumstances take a friend down a peg or two. Rather than indulging in an "I told you so" moment or joyful vindication, agape covers a multitude of sins (see 1 Peter 4:8). Agape realizes that "there but for the grace of God go I." Agape speaks the words of John Donne, "Any man's death diminishes me, because I am involved in Mankind; and therefore, never send to know for whom the bell tolls; it tolls for thee."[4] My friend's loss is my loss. I don't rejoice and cheer at her mistakes, missteps, or misfortune, because as my covenant friend, she is part of me. To rejoice in the wrong is to risk losing a friend. Agape will sorrow over a friend's wrongdoing and gently point the way to righteousness.

Now, let's ask that all-important question again: How do you lose a friend in a short amount of time? Be envious. Be proud and boastful. Be self-seeking. Hold a grudge and rejoice in wrongdoing. Those classic mistakes will drive away almost any friend. If these are mistakes you have made, this does not have to be the end of the story. You can still have a happy ending. What you learned to do wrong you can learn to do right.

14

Time to Grow Up

Everything I need to know about the struggles of friendship I learned in kindergarten, not as a student but as a substitute teacher. My instructors were five-year-olds, and the lessons they taught showed just how early these relationship mistakes begin to bloom.

1. *Every human being is born with the desire to record wrongs.* Kindergarten is the perfect place to see this. Though at this young age this desire is disguised as tattling, the principle is the same: Both are founded on the need to tell someone else's business and see them get what they deserve. "Mrs. Weird!" (The children could not say my name without a "d" on the end.) "Bobby is out of his chair." "Mrs. Weird, Sally isn't supposed to get a drink without asking." "Mrs. Weird, John is at the block center and he didn't finish his worksheet." When I naïvely tried to teach them about the importance of being a loyal friend, I was interrupted. "Mrs. Weird, Katy has her colors out while you're trying to talk." Somehow, they missed the point.

2. *Selfish ambition plagues even the very young.* The phrase *me first* was second only to *I'm telling*. Whether it was lining up

to leave the room or turning in homework, the future grown-ups wrangled for the best position. They cut in front of friends, gave persuasive speeches about why their table should go to recess first, and generally finagled for any advantage. Nowhere was this urge to be better than their friends more evident than when we played a phonics game. The loser's disappointment went unnoticed as the victor celebrated his moment of glory. Who knew correctly reading the word *bad* could feel so good?

3. *The human desire to get even is in full bloom by age five.* This I discovered when I pried one child from the headlock another initiated. In explaining why he choked his classmate, the little boy said, "He tripped me and it wasn't very nice." The gasping offender got the message.

4. *No wrongdoing is out of the reach of even the youngest in our human race.* In the three days I substituted, I saw jealousy, anger, hatred, arrogance, boasting, revenge, cheating, greed, lying, and envy. All the stuff of a great soap opera was played out in pigtails and blue jeans. Or as the Bible puts it, "The acts of the flesh are obvious" (Galatians 5:19), even in the very young. It was a harsh lesson in reality.

That isn't all I learned in kindergarten. I also saw the potential that resides inside every human soul to be a friend. The same child who pushed also shared. The one who wrestled made me a valentine. The compulsive tattlers were also contagious huggers and smilers. More stunning was the zeal each one of those littles had for hearing the daily Bible story and the eagerness in their voices as we talked about God and with God in prayer. The gentleness and sincerity of their prayers revealed the potential of a life yielded to God. Only through His intervention could a nature so bent on selfishness grow to be selfless. That is because "the sinful nature desires what is contrary to the Spirit, and the Spirit what is contrary to the sinful nature. They are in conflict with each other" (Galatians 5:17).

Thankfully, for those of us who still see glimpses of kindergarten conduct evident in our lives and our friendships, we can also rely on the Spirit to bring transformation. Paul reveals this is possible because

> Those who belong to Christ Jesus have nailed the passions and desires of their sinful nature to his cross and crucified them there. Since we are living by the Spirit, let us follow the Spirit's leading in every part of our lives. Let us not become conceited, or provoke one another, or be jealous of one another. (Galatians 5:24–26 NLT)

> The Holy Spirit produces this kind of fruit in our lives: love, joy, peace, patience, kindness, goodness, faithfulness, gentleness, and self-control. There is no law against these things! (Galatians 5:22–23 NLT)

For those of us who still see glimpses of kindergarten conduct evident in our lives and our friendships, we can also rely on the Spirit to bring transformation.

By giving the Spirit—instead of the flesh—control, He can replace our temptation to count wrongs and get even with self-control. We can overcome complaints with joy, selfish ambition with sacrificial love, and anger with patience and gentleness. In other words, with the help of the Spirit, we can grow up. That is good news when we are discouraged by the bad habits that have dominated our relationships. As we come to the concluding lessons of the love chapter, we find six expressions of agape that lead to and are required of mature and lasting friendships.

Friends Rejoice in Truth

"Agape rejoices with the truth."

From the Greek *alētheia*—what is true in things pertaining to God and the duties of man.

In this era of fake news, *The National Enquirer*, and 1-800-Psychic, the concept of absolute truth is an archaic ideal. These days, everyone is entitled to have and live according to their own truth. My truth doesn't have to be the same as your truth, because truth, in the modern context, is based on personal experience and preference. No wonder the world is disoriented and growing ever more chaotic. Where truth is a variable instead of an absolute, we are captive to the constantly changing whims of self. Jesus warned that only one thing can set us free: "If you hold to my teaching, you are really my disciples. Then you will know the truth, and the truth will set you free." (John 8:31–32).

Rejoicing in that kind of truth, cheering it, celebrating it, pursuing, and even guarding it is the key to growing past the bratty self that demands its own way. The ultimate truth is Jesus himself. He is the way, the truth, and the life (John 14:6). Truth begins with Him, but it does not end with Him. Instead, a relationship with Jesus is the door to every other bondage-breaking truth. His Word is where we open doors to discover what is true about Him, what is true about us, and what is true about this world and the world to come.

Truth is so foundational that Jesus said, "Those who worship Him must worship in spirit and truth" (John 4:24 NASB). It is a bedrock part of our relationship with Him, and now we discover it is bedrock in our relationship with each other. Truth is not just knowledge. It is truth pertaining to the duties (actions) of man. God does not say to merely know truth, but also to act on what we know to be true. Rejoicing in truth is a matter of *show and tell*, not just know and tell. Showing is action that flows from rejoicing that the truth we know is worthy to live by. Truth, though, should never act alone. Consider Tim Keller's words:

> Love without truth is sentimentality; it supports and affirms us but keeps us in denial about our flaws. Truth without love is harshness; it gives us information but in such a way that we cannot really hear it. God's saving love in Christ, however, is marked by both radical

truthfulness about who we are and yet also radical, unconditional commitment to us.[1]

That is the model of agape rejoicing in truth. When we are committed to radical truthfulness in the context of our agape commitment of friendship, it will shape more than how we feel. Truth will drastically impact how we act.

- We won't make assumptions, but actively seek the whole truth.
- We won't judge what we do not know.
- We will share transparently about our struggles.
- We will seek to understand others.
- We won't shrink back from sharing hard things, but always speak truth from a place of love.
- We won't wear masks to hide who we are, how we feel, or how we struggle.
- We will take time to discover the truth of a person's character, not judging a book by the cover.
- We will always point others to the truths God's Word declares.
- We will own our mistakes rather than hide them.
- We will share truth to give hope in the hard seasons others endure.
- We will make the truth of the gospel the foundation of friendship.
- We will live the truth of the gospel as a living witness to our friends.
- We will not be ashamed of truth that is inconvenient to the culture.

You cannot be a fake and also be a friend who rejoices in the truth. Agape does not hide nor hedge. It doesn't jump to conclusions or make snap judgments. It loves the light of truth and makes every effort to bring that light into every aspect of relationship. Are you prepared to be a transparent, accountable, truth-seeking friend? That is agape.

Friends Always Protect

"Agape protects all things."

From the Greek *stegō*—to cover closely, to protect by covering, and then to conceal, and then, by covering, to bear up under.

The same Greek word Paul used here is sometimes translated "roof." I've had experience with roofs lately. We just had a messy roof leak. We live in a two-story house and had no idea there was a problem until water started pouring through the ceiling of the first floor. As empty-nesters, we had no one in the upper rooms to notice when the leak was a small matter. Instead, during a major deluge, I woke up to find it raining in my kitchen. The water flooded an upstairs bathroom first and then overflowed through to the first floor. We called a roofer three times, but he was so busy he kept canceling our appointment. With more rain coming, I took matters into my own hands. I bought a can of sealant and headed to the roof. I won't lie. It was scary. The pitch of our roof is incredibly steep and it is a long way down. Still, if I didn't cover the hole, minor damage had the potential to be extremely costly. With my husband at work, I determined to fix it before the rain began again. My daughter came over to make sure I didn't fall in the attempt, or at least to call 9-1-1 if I did.

"Mom, are you sure you don't want to wait for the roofer—or for Dad?"

With more confidence than I felt, I pronounced dramatically, "Who knows that I was not born for such a time as this. If I perish, I perish. I will protect my house!"

So up I went, gingerly scooching around on my backside in search of the hole, with the can of sealant in one hand and the other helping me resist gravity pulling me earthward. After a few minutes, I found where a roofing nail had worked its way through the shingles, leaving an unprotected gap. As more rain clouds gathered overheard, I sealed the hole. When the rains fell throughout the next week, the sealant worked like a charm, protecting us from more damage so we could make inside repairs.

> When we feel ourselves wanting to cajole, coach, or correct them, we can protect them by making our bond a higher priority than our preferences.

In simple terms, to be a friend is to be a roof over others, and sometimes to be a roofing contractor. When you enter into covenant friendship, you are saying, "I will protect you. I will put a cover over you and not let you be exposed to harm. I will take the risks of standing in the gap to protect you from exposure, ridicule, and harm." Agape doesn't gossip or put another's weaknesses on display. It keeps confidences, shoulders private struggles, accepts differences, and shields from ridicule. It bears all things while not baring anything.

Even if the issue is sin, agape makes every effort to stand guard so that the least amount of damage is done and repairs can take place. Agape does not defend or protect sin, but it protects the sinner and helps facilitate restoration. Paul painted the picture:

> If anyone is caught in any transgression, you who are spiritual should restore him in a spirit of gentleness. Keep watch on yourself, lest you too be tempted. Bear one another's burdens, and so fulfill the law of Christ. (Galatians 6:1–2 ESV)

If the offense is against you, protection means keeping it to yourself. Sometimes that is the hardest thing to bear, as we want comfort and affirmation when we are wronged. Yet broadcasting a friend's failure amounts to self-seeking indulgence that is costly to both you and your friend. Agape proceeds biblically, not dramatically. Jesus was clear:

> If your brother sins against you, go and tell him his fault, between you and him alone. If he listens to you, you have gained your brother. (Matthew 18:15)

Too often, what we feel is a sin against us is really just our inability to accept that our friend sees things differently, does things differently, or wants different things from us. That is not sin. That is preference. Here, too, agape protects. It guards the friend from demands to change or to conform to our preferences. It protects their right to be unique. When we feel ourselves wanting to cajole, coach, or correct them, we can protect them by making our bond a higher priority than our preferences. Here is Paul's challenge:

> Be completely humble and gentle; be patient, bearing with one another in love. Make every effort to keep the unity of the Spirit through the bond of peace. (Ephesians 4:2–3)

That is what it looks like to "count others more significant than yourselves" (Philippians 2:3 ESV). What if you are certain your opinion or preference is the right one? Paul wrote,

> Accept the one whose faith is weak, without quarreling over disputable matters. . . . Accept one another, then, just as Christ accepted you, in order to bring praise to God. (Romans 14:1; 15:7)

We are not called to make our friends over in our own image, but to love them for being image-bearers of God as He has created them to be. Accepting our friend with all her foibles brings praise to our heavenly Father. How great is that and what a relief that we are not responsible for changing them (or their minds). When the matter of contention is actually an offense, we can protect them best by taking our eyes off of them and looking first in a mirror. As Jesus said,

> Why do you look at the speck of sawdust in your brother's eye and pay no attention to the plank in your own eye? How can you say to

> your brother, "Let me take the speck out of your eye," when all the time there is a plank in your own eye? You hypocrite, first take the plank out of your own eye, and then you will see clearly to remove the speck from your brother's eye. (Matthew 7:3–5)

Agape knows with certainty that you were raised up for such a time as this, to be a friend who will protect, shield, and guard your friends.

Friends Always Believe; Friends Always Hope

> "Agape believes all things and hopes in all things."

From the Greek *pisteuō* and *elpizō*—to think to be true, to be persuaded of, to credit, and place confidence in; to wait in hope.

With young children to raise in a single-income family, hand-me-downs were part of our financial planning. My kids were used to wearing what siblings had outgrown. Anything not completely trashed at the end of our line, we passed to another family with kids younger than ours. We know the help was appreciated because we were so grateful when such things came our way. One friend in particular always passed down items that were nicer than what we bought new. She kept everything in pristine condition and then found joy in being able to make them a blessing to another family. I got a call one day that she had some things she thought our son might like. I told him about the call at dinner.

"Honey, Mrs. Kathy called today and said she has a blazer she wants to give you. Would you like to have it?"

"Wow, Mom. That is so generous. I won't even have my driver's license for four years!"

After a moment of confusion, I realized his misunderstanding.

"She has a blazer *jacket* to give you, not a Chevy Blazer, babe."

He was disappointed, but how telling that his view of our friend was in no way incompatible with the possibility of such an extravagant gift. That is what agape friendship should look like.

It is a generous belief in the goodness of friends. It always gives them the benefit of the doubt. It believes the best, not the worst.

Agape is not a gullible love. It will not be fooled into believing what is false, turning a blind eye to the truth. Agape abides in truth, but it also abides in trust. Agape rejects suspicion, doubt, pessimism, or cynicism. It takes words at face value instead of imputing negative meanings. If the need arises, it subscribes to "innocent until proven guilty." If there is any doubt, friendship comes down on the side of trust. It doesn't demand to be convinced or to cross-examine to find fault. One commentary writer put it this way: "When Love has no evidence, it believes the best. When the evidence is adverse, it hopes for the best. And when hopes are repeatedly disappointed, it still courageously waits."[2] Covenant friendship comes down to trust that hopes love will bear fruit.

Friends Always Persevere

> "Agape always perseveres."

From the Greek *hypomenō*—to remain, not recede or flee; to persevere under misfortunes and trials; to endure, bear bravely and calmly.

Being a picky eater is part of my identity and has been since I was a child defiantly refusing to eat a chicken pot pie. I'd sooner have fled the table than eat exotic foods like brussels sprouts and lima beans. At the top of the list of my food phobias is anything that once lived in water. If the entire body of a critter can fit on a plate, it was not meant to be eaten. That is my policy; or it was before I went to foreign lands to encourage new friends in Christ.

The place that irreversibly changed my identity as a picky eater was Cyprus. A first stop for many refugees from the Middle East and Africa, this little island country in the Mediterranean Sea is home to the nations. I use the term *home* loosely; many displaced people reside there, but home is someplace most will never see again. Being invited to share their meal is more than a matter of hospitality. It is an expression of their identity. With resolve and a prayer that I would not disgrace myself, I had Persian food with Persians, Lebanese food with Syrians and Lebanese, Greek food with Greek Cypriots, and Turkish food with Turkish Cypriots.

Only one test remained—the dreaded fish. The missionary friends hosting me said I could not truly identify with the island culture unless I embraced fish. What was set before me was my greatest fear: the entire fish body, head to tailfin. My resolve almost faltered under the unblinking stare of my food looking up at me, but my hosts were watching expectantly. With an apology uttered to the fish's face, I did what I would never do at home—I ate the fish.

Friends do not flee the table when they don't like what is being served. They remain, and more than that, agape friends pick up the fork. They remain actively involved when served hardships, challenges, suffering, pain, loneliness, persecution, and ingratitude. When the going gets tough, the tough stay put—and get engaged. Agape friends do not merely put up with circumstances, they press in. Ruth is a friend who remained at the table, but she did more than sit on her hands; she made the most of what was served. Circumstances served her mother-in-law, Naomi, deprivation, so Ruth remained to work. Naomi was served loneliness, so Ruth remained with companionship. Naomi was served despair; Ruth remained to give hope. There is restoration power in remaining with a friend through the hard places and even through the hard seasons of your relationship. Perseverance shouts loudly, "You are worth the struggle!"

Friends Never Fail

"Agape never fails."

From the Greek *piptō*—to come to an end, disappear, cease.

If by now you are wondering how you could ever be a friend who embodies all the qualities required of love, please let me assure you—you can't. At least, you can't by mere human effort. These aspects of friendship originate in divine love, not human effort. This is a portrait of Jesus' friendship to us. As we replace "love" in the recounting of chapter 13 with "Jesus," who is love, we see an amazing picture.

> Jesus is patient, Jesus is kind. He does not envy, He does not boast, He is not proud. Jesus does not dishonor others, He is not self-seeking, He is not easily angered, He keeps no record of wrongs. Jesus does not delight in evil but rejoices with the truth. Jesus always protects, always trusts, always hopes, always perseveres. Jesus never fails.

Remember the love chapter started by making clear that human effort amounts to nothing by itself. That is also where the chapter ends. Everything of this world is temporary, even supernatural gifts. Agape is the pursuit that transcends time and eternity. That is why agape love is our greatest pursuit. Consider these conclusions:

> Where there are prophecies, they will cease; where there are tongues, they will be stilled; where there is knowledge, it will pass away. For we know in part and we prophesy in part, but when completeness comes, what is in part disappears. When I was a child, I talked like a child, I thought like a child, I reasoned like a child. When I became a man, I put the ways of childhood behind me. For now, we see only a reflection as in a mirror; then we shall see face to face. Now I know in part; then I shall know fully, even as I am fully known. And now these three remain: faith, hope and [agape]. But the greatest of these is [agape]. (1 Corinthians 13:8–13)

Paul wrote that challenging call to agape love knowing full well that we have no power to live it out successfully:

> Not that we are competent in ourselves to claim anything for ourselves, but our competence comes from God. He has made us competent as ministers of a new covenant. (2 Corinthians 3:5–6)

Once we realize how inadequate we truly are, we can admit it to Jesus and ask for help. "Lord, I can't be a friend like you. I am too weak and too selfish. Help me, please." You can have confidence that it is God's purpose that we friend like Him. It is for His sake, so we can reveal His good nature as a Friend. He delights to help us because He delights in bringing about His will. That's why we have this promise:

> This is the confidence we have in approaching God: that if we ask anything according to his will, he hears us. And if we know that he hears us—whatever we ask—we know that we have what we asked of him. (1 John 5:14–15)

In fact, He has already prepared to help us by giving us a Friend on the inside:

> I will ask the Father, and he will give you another advocate to help you and be with you forever—the Spirit of truth. The world cannot accept him, because it neither sees him nor knows him. But you know him, for he lives with you and will be in you. (John 14:16–17)

Little in your life is as important as allowing the Holy Spirit to grow you into the kind of friend to others that Jesus is to us. Agape is how we walk "worthy of the calling we have received" (Ephesians 4:1). You will never love your friends perfectly, but continually surrendering your rights and wants will increasingly bring maturity. Oh, my dear sister, the rewards are worth all the ways you will die to yourself for others. You cannot have friends unless you are ready to do some friending.

Whether you desire to friend someone older or younger, someone like you or completely different, a husband, a daughter, a sister, or a stranger, these qualities of love will bear fruit when diligently practiced in partnership with God himself. As you depend on Him, agape can become what you are known for among all those who count you a friend. Go ahead. Insert your name and then ask God to help you live up to the great and beautiful calling of loving as He loves.

_______ is patient, _______ is kind. _______ does not envy, _______ does not boast, _______ is not proud. _______ does not dishonor others, _______ is not self-seeking, _______ is not easily angered, _______ keeps no record of wrongs. _______ does not delight in evil but rejoices with the truth. _______ always protects, always trusts, always hopes, always perseveres. _______ never fails. _______ is an agape friend.

15

The Care and Feeding of Friends

When we allowed our daughter to adopt a sassy llama she found on the internet, my husband was adamant that President O'llama would be the final animal to join the herd. Already in the menagerie was a horse, dogs, cats, birds, and a pig. He was drawing the line. Then Hannah's friend gave her a snake as a Christmas present. How do you refuse a gift?! A week later, I arrived home to find that her new reptilian pet had pets. Two live mice were added to the snake's cage to be his dinner, but after three days the snake still hadn't eaten them. Instead, his dinner became our regular dinner guests, requiring care and feeding to keep them plump and delicious. While the mouse drama was still playing out, Hannah came home with a refugee rabbit whose owner couldn't keep it.

"Don't worry," she reassured. "I'm not keeping Gibbs. I'll find him a good home."

That seemed doubtful. Our daughter spent the weekend improving the living situations of not just the rabbit but also the mice. When I questioned this, she had an explanation.

"I thought I should make them comfortable until the snake gets hungry."

Instead of death row, Romeo and Juliet (yes, they got names) moved into a luxury mouse condo. If you build a mouse a house, he will make himself at home. The snake, henceforth, dined only on frozen rats. I received no explanation for Gibbs's upgraded quarters, just that look I've seen so many times before. They were no longer visitors. Hannah had bonded. She gave them names. She bought them food and built them homes. She was all in.

Sister, we have to be all in when it comes to the care and feeding of our friendships. These are not casual visitors to our lives. Each one needs to be fed its own unique blend of time, emotional energy, companionship, and personal investment. Each needs a special place to be at home with us. Friendships are living things that thrive only if we care for them. Left to fend for themselves, they will quickly perish. (I'll spare you the Wier pet stories that illustrate that point.)

Taking time to assess how a relationship is growing and what it needs is important. Here are three specific areas to regularly evaluate.

Communication

When asked that all-too-common question "How are you?" do you tell the whole truth?

For one brief second, you might consider actually responding with how you truly are—tired, sad, stressed, excited, overwhelmed, depressed, proud, hopeful, hopeless, confused, confident, lonely, and/or all of the above. It is such a huge question to be so simple. You have so much you could share—so much you need to share.

And then it occurs to you—they likely don't want to know how you are *really* doing. In fact, it might scare them to know how you are doing. At the very least, that kind of honesty makes people uncomfortable. So conforming to social etiquette, you answer, "Fine, how are you?"

That is probably only fair. What are the chances you want the details of their lives any more than they want the details of yours? To truly care about friends, and to care about the potential to create meaningful friendships, you have to care about the details—and that means you have to move to substantive conversation. That may seem like a small step toward friendship, but remember, the longing of friendship is really a longing to be known.

Asking questions is the best way to know the heart of another person. Whether you are talking to your close friend or a new acquaintance, you can open new doors with deliberate inquiries. Targeted questions lead to transparent honesty. Instead of "How are you?" why not, "What's weighing on your mind today?" In a world of lonely people struggling to bear up under daily pressures, feeding them interested questions can help build your emotional bonds. Ponder how you might answer these and what you might learn if you asked them of others.

Is today a good day for you, or has it been difficult?

Do you have any big deadlines or projects on your plate right now?

What challenging things are ahead for you?

Are you having to put out any fires in your life right now?

What have you enjoyed about parenting recently?

What has been difficult in this season of parenting?

What new goals are you working on?

What three words describe your life right now?

What memorable things have happened in your life recently?

What would you like a re-do on?

What has made you grow lately?

Are you intimidated by anything in your life right now?

What are you doing to relax these days?

What is your creative outlet?
Have you started anything new?
What is keeping you up at night?
How do you deal with stress?
What have you learned this year that has really helped you?
Do you feel like you have enough time in your day?
Where do you dream of putting your talents to use?
Where have you seen God working in your life?
Where would you like God to work in your life?

A friendship cannot grow if you don't also include one more question: *Can I share one of my struggles with you?* Asking others to be transparent while holding back your true self can never lead to intimacy because it undermines trust. *You must tell me all your secrets but I don't trust you enough to tell you mine.* That is not transparency. It is only availability. You are offering your attention, empathy, support, and encouragement in exchange for their transparency. Until you open up, you are not offering your friendship. Even then, transparency is more than just spilling your guts. According to David Kinnaman, president of the Barna Research Group,

> The motivation of transparency is important. The culture teaches people to be candid and blunt, but this usually revolves around self-centeredness—you have a right to express your true feelings and your rage. This is an entitlement. Instead, the Christian way to approach transparency is to realize our candidness should be motivated by a desire to have a pure heart before God and others.[1]

We don't share to create or reinforce an image. We share to create fellowship. It flows like this:

> If we walk in the light, as he is in the light, we have fellowship with one another, and the blood of Jesus his Son cleanses us from all sin. (1 John 1:7)

You have to give transparency, not just receive it, to let the light into your relationship. That means you have to take a risk. Mother Teresa noted, "Honesty and transparency make you vulnerable. Be honest and transparent anyway."[2] When you open up about your own struggles, aspirations, and emotions, you risk judgment, apathy, and even rejection. You also open the door to intimacy, connection, affirmation, understanding, and support. The risk is big but the rewards are bigger. For our part, we can do two things to foster relationships built on vulnerability and transparency so that fellowship can grow. If your relationships are floundering, start evaluating your communication in these areas.

Asking others to be transparent while holding back your true self can never lead to intimacy because it undermines trust.

First, be the safe and trustworthy place for your friends to be honest. Jesus is our model. He knew the deepest secrets of His friends' hearts and guarded them with wisdom. The woman at the well who had multiple husbands. Zacchaeus the tax collector who cheated and stole. The woman caught in adultery. The lepers cast out by society. Peter who fearfully denied Jesus. Misunderstood Martha. The rich young man who idolized his possessions. Nicodemus, who had an identity crisis. In each case, Jesus did not pull back from the messy disclosures. He pressed in with love, compassion, understanding, and truth. He touched. He listened. He asked questions. He fellowshiped. He protected. When He counseled, He did so gently. When He admonished, He did so lovingly. No one walked away from Jesus shamed by His response or sorry they had been honest. He could be trusted with full disclosure without the risk of rejection. That is the kind of safety and acceptance we all long to experience. Be the one to give it.

The second thing we can do to foster vulnerability and transparency is to be honest *first*. Ernest Hemingway said, "The best way to find out if you can trust somebody is to trust them first."[3] Transparency cannot survive without trust, but somebody has to start that ball rolling. Our willingness to make the first move is itself an act of trust, as well as an offer for the other person to reciprocate. If we are not willing to trust someone, don't expect to receive their trust. So now we're back to vulnerability and risk.

> Transparency cannot survive without trust, but somebody has to start that ball rolling.

In investing, risk tolerance is the amount of market ups and downs an investor can stomach. It's used to decide whether an investor will be aggressive, moderate, or conservative in growing capital. As you try to grow relationships, you probably need to know your risk tolerance. The more you hold back, the less return you can expect. If you are willing to invest greater vulnerability, the payoff will be a truly full relationship. But there is no way to mitigate all risk. Relationship pain will happen, but as you pray and proceed with wisdom, the risk can also result in deeper, more honest friendships, characterized by the light of truth.

Balance of Power

I am a bit of a political junkie. I follow politics because whoever is in charge has the most leverage when making policy. Every two years I'm on pins and needles with the rest of the country to see how elections will shift the balance—and it shifts often. Pundits tell you that fluidity is a healthy check on power. You know the old saying: Power corrupts, and absolute power corrupts absolutely. The same is true when it comes to friendship. When power is out of balance, our relationships can be corrupted. There are two areas where balance in friendship is relevant: a balanced variety of friendships, and a balance of power in our most equitable friendships.

First, let's consider variety. It goes without saying that no two friendships will be the same. Levels of intimacy, availability, history, and even camaraderie vary from relationship to relationship. Variety is part of the blessing of investing in more than one bestie. It is what makes the mosaic of friends so beautiful. My friend Mary's artwork is so spectacular because no two elements that make up her finished mixed-media portraits are the same. Each item within the portrait, whether a piece of tile or a straw or a small Hot Wheels car, adds in a unique way to the beauty of the whole. Uniformity paints a dull picture. We should not want or expect each friend to contribute to our life in the same way. When we are able to celebrate each relationship for its uniqueness, we will also set each free of burdensome expectations.

Enjoy your quirky friend without lamenting that she isn't serious enough. Embrace your serious friend and stop trying to make her lighten up. Go deep with your deep friends, go adventuring with your adventurous friends, and be happy to catch up by text with your busy, overwhelmed friend. As you begin to celebrate each relationship for what it is, you will begin to enjoy them more without the pressure that comes with comparison.

Within that mosaic, not only do we want friendships with unique character, but we also want them to have variety in purpose. I loathe exercise. I don't find it invigorating or enjoyable. I do, however, need it. I was diagnosed with severe early onset osteoporosis. The doctor warned me that if I don't begin a regimen of strength training, I will one day be a little old lady with a hunched back. My solution to this problem has been finding a variety of people who can motivate me in different ways.

The first person I sought out was a trainer. I need someone with expertise to teach me and to push me to do better. I also found that I made progress by inviting a friend who hates exercise even more than I do to come along on the improvement journey. When we are together, I cheer her on, teach her what I have already learned, and keep step with her to encourage her not to quit. I may not have a ton of expertise, but I am able to share what I have to spur her on to better health. I'm also on the fitness journey with a friend who is addressing her own health issues. Since we are in the same boat, we encourage each other and relate to the setbacks and the victories. The overall strategy, then, is to get help, to give help, and to help each other. That is the variety we need in our friendships: a friend to learn from, a friend to teach, and one who walks where we walk.

We should have at least one friend who is further down the road spiritually and experientially than we are. We need their wisdom and experience as a guide. It doesn't have to be an official mentoring relationship with scheduled meetings and book studies. Living alongside someone who has demonstrated faithfulness and maturity will yield many lessons along the way.

Several years ago I joined a prayer group that meets weekly to pray for missionaries. This group has been meeting in the same home for fifty years. Before I joined with another friend, the youngest person in the group was in her eighties. The group leader, Dottie, had just turned one hundred. The group has been faithful to God and to one another for decades, and they welcomed Susan and me as if we were daughters (or granddaughters). Their hard-learned wisdom, always shared generously, has been a lamp to us as younger women in many of our own trials. In addition to learning more about the privilege of prayer by simply participating with them, they have also mentored us in hospitality, kindness, love in action, faith, counting it all joy, perspective, and perseverance. They have tutored us in the deeper things that only those who have camped in deep valleys can teach. Each one has experienced painful trials, yet endured without a hint of bitterness or guile.

Thanks to this gang of gray ladies, I am growing in faith, hope, and love. They know we can't give to them what they give to us, but we are embraced as friends who receive more than we give. I love them as much as I have loved any friend of any age. Relationships may be different, but the character of love is the same.

I don't have a hundred years of experience, but I can share what I do have with the women coming behind me who need a guide.

A young mom struggling in a season of being overwhelmed. A woman who desires to know God's Word in a more personal way. A wife who is being tested in her marriage. Those who follow in paths we have walked need what we are able to give—perspective, hope, and biblical truth all in the context of friendship.

As a women's ministry director, I could clearly see that this need within our church was great. In counsel with two other women, we began to pray that God would make these relationships a reality for our women. The end result was a new ministry we named FFE, Friends for Eternity. Our hope was to connect women in eternally significant ways that crossed the normal barriers of age and interest. Meeting once a month, we created fellowship groups that give younger women (twenty- to forty-year-olds) regular meaningful access to older women (over forty).

The outcome has been beyond what we expected. The younger women gain godly perspective from more experienced women. The older women answer the call to teach matters of life to younger women. I have grown to deeply love the five younger women who are part of my own group that is in its fifth year. We have formed close bonds as these unbalanced friendships flourish, and we are no longer just friends in a fellowship group. We are friends indeed. Just because relationships are unbalanced does not mean they are unsatisfying. God blesses those who give in equal measure to those we give to. We expected He would because such imbalanced relationships are also part of His friendship calling to us. Paul explained it this way:

> Warn those who are lazy. Encourage those who are timid. Take tender care of those who are weak. Be patient with everyone. (1 Thessalonians 5:14 NLT)

Perhaps the person you tenderly care for will be a peer who is simply at the maximum margins of her life and needs support. It might be a friend navigating a deep valley, someone with a difficult personality, or a person who needs a model of maturity. It need not be a formal group. God will lead you to a friend who needs what you have to give and who doesn't have much to offer in return right now. Don't run from that relationship. It can be a beautiful part of the mosaic God is painting for you.

There is another kind of variety that is important to strive for as you invest in others. While there is no true equality in friendship, there should be some balanced friendships. Those would be relationships where two maturing friends are both committed to investing in each other, sacrificing for each other, and spending time with each other. Both bring a healthy sense of self and purpose to the table and are able to "spur one another on toward love and good deeds" (Hebrews 10:24). It is a friendship of mutuality. These relationships are essential. They give you the opportunity to give and receive together. Mutuality lets you share your opinion without it being received as superior. It lets you be honest about weakness without feeling inferior. It is a friendship where the responsibility for intimacy is shared. No one party does the heavy lifting. The friendship is equally refreshing to both.

A mutual friendship will not be dominated by one person. It will be a fluid give and take. Sometimes you give more and sometimes you receive more. Maturity allows the give and take to respond to the greater needs of the moment. What keeps the relationship healthy is compromise, concession, and good communication. But even these relationships can get out of balance. That is not the time to get self-conscious or offended. It is the time to be proactive. Consider how some of these actions might restore balance in a teetering friendship.

- Ask a busy friend who hasn't had time for you if you can come over and help her with something that is on her plate. Or if you are too busy, invite her to come help with a task while you catch up.
- Be the first to forgive a misunderstanding.
- Let your friend have the spotlight.

- Offer to drive even though your friend always says she doesn't mind.
- Meet for an hour of share and prayer.
- Take the initiative in planning time together.
- Consider ways your friend invests in you that perhaps you have overlooked.

Simple acts of care can help get a mature relationship back into balance. Each is unique, so there isn't a one-size-fits-all fix when things are out of balance. Still, there are some trusted remedies.

First, don't panic or get your feelings hurt. Take time to assess where you are and how you got there. Pray. Pray some more. Search your own heart to make sure you are not projecting insecurity into the situation. Pray. Consider what action you can take on your part to restore the balance. Give where you need to give. Communicate with your friend. Don't assume she is aware that the balance has changed and already knows you are concerned. Ask questions. Don't accuse. Be kind. Pray. Make allowances for demands in your friend's life that could be affecting her availability. Be a friend. Be prepared, knowing that friendships go through seasons. If this friendship needs space, resist resentment by intentionally thanking God for how the friendship has blessed you. Leave the door open, but lean into other relationships. There is only so much of you, and gaining margin in your emotional and physical availability can be an opportunity to grow a relationship that hasn't had as much of your attention. Move expectantly in that direction while keeping a wide-open door to the relationship that needs a little space for the time being.

Expiration Date

I am notorious for keeping items in my pantry long past the expiration date. I beat my own record last year when I found a can of baking powder in the back of the pantry that expired in 2008.

I used it anyway. Predictably, my Texas chocolate sheet cake was flat. When we try to make things work that are past expiration, the results will disappoint. We know what it means to say that friendships can expire. It happens for many reasons. We enter different life seasons. One person grows spiritually and the other drifts. A past hurt caused damage that didn't heal. Moves, marriages, maturity.

Relationships are always at risk of becoming perishable. That's why we feed and care for them. But even then, some friendships will have a shorter shelf life. I made a list of the twenty-five most pivotal mutual friendships in my life, going back as far as my later school years. Of the twenty-five gals, only six remain in my life in a meaningful way. I moved away from some. Some moved away from me. One put distance between us as she drifted from her own faithfulness to God. One relationship, which I already told you about, I killed myself. One friend got so lost in a personal crisis that she closed everyone out. Two never grew in maturity as they grew in age, and while we still connect occasionally, they are no longer mutual relationships. I stay connected on Facebook with three who relocated, but we haven't maintained our personal connections. One dear friend relocated to heaven.

Of the six who have remained in my life, I haven't lived in the same town with three of them for more than twenty years, yet those friendships have not expired just because of distance. Each is still vitally significant. The same can be said of a dear friend who moved just two years ago. We continue building into each other's lives, just not day to day. My two closest local friends have endured in intimacy and transparency, while other local relationships have ebbed. There is nothing alarming in any of that.

Friendships have seasons. I have had many come and go. I know you have too. Even the relationships we maintain don't remain the same. So with all this change, how do we find equilibrium? Here are my suggestions for letting go when that season of fellowship has come to an end.

1. *Give yourself the freedom to feel the loss.* No matter what the reason is, when distance moves in, it usually brings sadness.

Lament is a healthy process. Go ahead and take time to feel the loss now so that you don't take your sorrow into the next season with you.

2. *Don't let it define you.* This is vitally relevant if a friend has quit your relationship. Rejection has the potential to make us feel worthless. Dear sister, that is a lie. You are infinitely valuable. Even in those cases where you make mistakes, you are God's wonderful workmanship—even as a work in progress. Be *confident* of this: He who began a good work in you will carry it on to completion until the day of Christ Jesus (Philippians 1:6). Pick your head up. You bear the image of your Creator. You are not defined by who likes you, but by Who loves you.

Pick your head up. You bear the image of your Creator. You are not defined by who likes you, but by Who loves you.

3. *Be thankful.* In the midst of counting your loss, count your blessings. Thank God for all the ways you were blessed by the friendship. There is no expiration on the investment God made in you through your friend. Specifically, thank God for the qualities of your friend that made your life better. Thank Him for the opportunities you had to love her well.

4. *Be prayerful.* Pray for your friend to turn toward God, and find comfort in the loss. When an earthly friendship ebbs, it is a powerful reminder that you have a friend who will never leave you or forsake you. Refresh yourself by renewing that friendship. If you have bitterness taking root, confess it to God and ask Him to heal the wound and help you not to count the wrong.

5. *Evaluate the beginning and the ending.* When you are in a healthy emotional and spiritual mind-set, step back and consider the expired friendship. How did it begin? Was it healthy? What paths did it take? Was it centered on truth and transparency? Is there any aspect of the relationship that teaches you lessons for the future?

6. *Let go gracefully.* Whether it is distance or hard circumstances that separate you from a close friend, you can choose to let go gracefully. Foremost, remember that you are a covenant friend. Your commitment outlasts time and circumstance. That means you have to think about the other person's experience and release your me-first mind-set, even at the close of your companionship. How can you offer comfort in the loss? In what ways can you extend an olive branch so that wounds can heal? How can you set a guard on your tongue to protect her reputation even if you have been wronged? Letting go gracefully can mean trusting God with your reputation while preserving hers. Your covenant is to be a faithful friend no matter what—even when the season of being together concludes. Love remains even when fellowship ends.

7. *Expect God to fill the space.* Remind yourself that God desires that you live in mutual affection with others. He created you to be an *us*. He looked at aloneness and declared it not good. You can confidently place your hope for mutual life-giving relationships in God's hands and look forward with expectancy to the joy of new relationships. We can confidently take Paul's advice:

> Command those who are rich in this present world not to be arrogant nor to put their hope in wealth, which is so uncertain, but to put their hope in God, who richly provides us with everything for our enjoyment. (1 Timothy 6:17)

When new doors open, remember that agape friendship is the way to make a relationship thrive so you enjoy it to the fullest.

16

How Does Your Garden Grow?

Always up for a challenge, I decided to follow in my mother's footsteps and grow a garden. She has always had a green thumb and can grow a bounty of produce on a small plot of earth. My husband questioned the wisdom of my plan, reminding me that I have a black thumb and that no houseplant has ever survived my loving care.

"That's true," I confessed. "But I am going to grow plants outside."

For the next three days, my kids helped me weed, till, hoe, and plant. This required an investment of about five hundred dollars, since I needed a tiller, a new shovel, a hoe, gloves, and seedlings to make our experimental garden a reality. The experiment was whether someone as inept as I am at gardening could actually get food to grow by following established gardening principles.

The first thing harvested was a single yellow squash. It was beautiful, and I was so proud. That night I sautéed it and served it to my husband at dinner. It was a small squash, so there was only enough for one serving—which was actually fine since I don't eat squash.

"Well?" I asked eagerly, watching for his delight. "Is it fabulous?"

"It's the best five-hundred-dollar squash I've ever had," he said with a smile.

It was a lot of money and effort for just one smallish squash, but then again, how can you put a price on the value of teamwork, effort, and family bonding we experienced in the process? Besides, I was optimistic that given time, a big crop would eventually grow.

A few days later we left for vacation and hired a young neighbor to water our garden. When we returned in ten days, we found a complete transformation. The garden overflowed with vegetables—and weeds. My optimism soared. It would be a wait for most of the produce to mature, but within fourteen days I harvested the makings of a single bowl of salad. I had fresh lettuce, a cucumber, and one bell pepper. I carefully arranged my bounty in a bowl, paused to photograph my accomplishment, and prepared to eat the best salad I had ever tasted.

Let's just say it was the best salad I had ever grown. The lettuce was stemmy and the pepper was tough—but the cucumber was delicious! It was a satisfying meal that had nothing to do with the flavor and everything to do with the accomplishment. Even better, we were down to one hundred dollars per vegetable grown, which was the best we would do since I failed to tend the garden and the weeds choked everything else out.

If you calculate the value strictly on the basis of the amount of produce yielded from our garden, you might say it was a bust. A single cucumber, a squash, a couple of peppers, and some lettuce hardly seem worth the investment we made. On the other hand, we proved that even the most inexperienced gardeners can succeed by adhering to a pattern that, if followed properly, is guaranteed to produce at least a small harvest. The experiment taught us much for our next attempt.

This is the same way we ought to approach sowing the seeds of new friendships. In a way, it is experimental. You now have reliable, established principles to follow, but what grows will depend on how you apply those principles in the real world and how diligently you tend the process. You will have to make an investment. You will have to put in an effort. You will have to trust God to do more than you can do by yourself.

In his classic book *The Celebration of Discipline*, Richard Foster reminds us how the process works.

> A farmer is helpless to grow grain; all he can do is provide the right conditions for the growing of grain. He cultivates the ground, he plants the seed, he waters the plants, and then the natural forces of the earth take over, and up comes the grain. This is the way it is with the Spiritual Disciplines—they are a way of sowing to the Spirit. The Disciplines are God's way of getting us into the ground; they put us where he can work within us and transform us. By themselves the Spiritual Disciplines can do nothing; they can only get us to the place where something can be done. They are God's means of grace.[1]

Foster did not list friendship as a spiritual discipline, but I believe it is. Just as Jesus practiced solitude and simplicity, worship and fasting to draw near to His Father, He also practiced friendship. In the discipline of building intimate relationships, Jesus fulfilled purposes God had for Him. In a prayer to His Father, He said,

> I have revealed you to those whom you gave me out of the world. They were yours; you gave them to me and they have obeyed your word. Now they know that everything you have given me comes from you. For I gave them the words you gave me and they accepted them. They knew with certainty that I came from you, and they believed that you sent me. (John 17:6–8)

We have been called to walk in that kind of friendship, having the spiritual discipline to reveal God to those He brings into our lives. When God has called us to something, He will meet us in it. As you take steps to till the ground and sow the seeds, remember, it is not all on your shoulders. You're only the farmer. Your role is to provide the right conditions for the fruit of friendship to grow. It starts by being the seed that dies to self. Then soften the ground with initiation, demonstration, and communication. Surrender joyfully to personal transformation. Above all, saturate your efforts with supplication. Without dependence on God, your friendships will have little chance of growing beyond the garden variety the world can produce. A friendship cultivated from your knees will produce fruit that lasts. You might begin here:

> God, satisfy me fully with your friendship so that I won't try to replace you. Change and heal my own heart that I might love who I am as you created me to be. Prepare hearts to receive what I have to offer. Give me eyes to see those you have prepared. Give me courage to be transparent and vulnerable. Help me see the needs that others don't express. Bring opportunities to show friendship with love. Give me a thankful heart for the people in my life. Inspire me with creative ways to reflect your friendship. Guard my mind that I would not be easily offended. Help me surrender my emotions to you as I initiate with others.
>
> As I love others well, help me trust you to bring those who will love me well with your love. Remind me often that being a friend is being about your business, not just mine. Thank you that your love shows me every day what life-giving friendship is meant to be. Amen.

Making and keeping biblical covenant friendships is not a simple matter of do's and don'ts. It is a spiritual discipline of surrendering your self-interests to show God's sacrificial agape love to others. It is divine in nature, so it must be dependent on the Divine. Imagine the kinds of friendships that will result with God's guiding and empowering.

Now it is time to consider again the people list you created when we began this conversation. Those are the relationships you have already started cultivating. Some are merely seedlings, but those acquaintances or casual friends have the potential to be so much more, given the right care. Close friends can become true inner-circle friends who share your innermost soul as you begin to cultivate them in a new and greater way.

> Without dependence on God, your friendships will have little chance of growing beyond the garden variety the world can produce. A friendship cultivated from your knees will produce fruit that lasts.

You cannot turn every connection into a significant covenant friendship, but it is unlikely that you are really starting from zero. Ask God to help you identify three people on that list with whom you can intentionally begin to initiate a deeper relationship. Spend a few days praying for them and for your desire to grow your relationship with them. Consider what they might most need from a friend right now. Then do it! Step out in faith and make the first move. You are going to be an incredible blessing in their lives as you make it your purpose to friend them the way Jesus has friended you.

Now that you have a new vision of friendship, consider how you might show agape in each encounter you have from those in your inner circle to mere acquaintances. Pray over all the names on your list as the days and weeks go by. Thank God again for every person. As you become intentional in every interaction, you will become more and more satisfied because you are growing as a friend. That is where you will find lasting satisfaction. Jesus did not declare that He accomplished what God desired because people liked Him. He was satisfied because He had loved well those God had entrusted to Him.

My dear sister, the real art of friendship is not in having many friends. It is accepting the challenge to follow in our Father's footsteps and to be a friend to as many as God brings into your life.

Don't despise small beginnings. What is small in your eyes is great in God's. The great theologian Charles Spurgeon reminds us that this too is one of God's upside-down realities:

> It is a very great folly to despise "the day of small things," for it is usually God's way to begin His great works with small things. We see it every day, for the first dawn of light is but feeble, and yet by and by, it grows into the full noontide heat and glory. . . . How tiny is the seed that is sown in the garden, yet out of it there comes the lovely flower! . . . Woe unto that man who despises "the day of small things" in the Church of Christ, or who despises "the day of smart things" in any individual believer, for it is God's day, it is a day out of which great things will yet come.[2]

Great things will come from your desire to have friends when it is rooted in your faithful practice of being a friend. That can happen this very day. Waiting for friendship ends the moment you step out to be the friend everyone else is praying God will send.

Acknowledgments

With gratitude, I sing the praises of those who contributed toward honoring God with this project. Coincidentally, most are new friends God brought into my circle while creating this book. Thank you to Ginger Kolbaba for bringing your skills as you edited these pages. Your careful eye and gift for clear communication helped focus the message and remove distractions. Thank you, Andy McGuire, for your enthusiasm and guidance. Appreciation goes to my agent, Don Gates of the Gates Group, for partnering to bring the messages on my heart to the hearts of others. And to the last of my new friends, thank you to the team at Baker and Bethany House who have contributed to sharing the message of artful friending with those who long for life-sharing relationships.

I also offer thanks to my friends and family who cared for me as I met deadlines. Thanks, Mom, for bringing meals so we wouldn't starve while I worked, for giving input, and mostly for being the friend every daughter hopes to have in a mom! Thanks to my husband for knowing with certainty that I loved him even while I was ignoring him to write. To my dear friends who encouraged, proofed, offered feedback, and prayed. To my kids, for not incurring disasters when I had deadlines to meet. And especially to all those women—both family and friends—who have taught me what it means to be a friend like Christ. Many of you are mentioned in these pages, but not all. Oh, how I love sharing my life with you.

Notes

Chapter 2 Knowing Up from Down

1. Randy Alcorn, *Heaven* (Carol Stream, IL: Tyndale, 2004), 54.

Chapter 3 Friends Not Fads

1. Martha Edwards, "Women and Friendships: Why We Are Falling Behind in Keeping Up Our Social Lives," *Huffington Post Canada*, September 28, 2011, https://www.huffingtonpost.ca/2011/09/26/women-friends_n_982245.html.

2. Edwards, "Women and Friendships."

Chapter 4 Filling the Tank

1. Gail O'Day, "I Have Called You Friends," Center for Christian Ethics at Baylor University, 2008, 21, https://www.baylor.edu/content/services/document.php/61118.pdf.

2. Gail O'Day, "I Have Called You Friends."

Chapter 6 Friend Yourself

1. *Nobel Ape* television special, produced by Comedy Dynamics, featuring Jim Gaffigan, aired July 13, 2018, on Comedy Central.

2. Jim Gaffigan, "Ask Jim Gaffigan," *Washington Post*, November 28, 2007, http://www.washingtonpost.com/wp-dyn/content/discussion/2007/11/27/DI2007112701770.html.

Chapter 7 This Is Us

1. "Girl Talk: The New Rules of Female Friendship and Communication," Social Issues Research Center, http://www.sirc.org/publik/girl_talk.shtml. For the full report, see http://www.sirc.org/publik/girl_talk.pdf.

Chapter 9 Till Death Do Us Part

1. L. M. Montgomery, *Anne of Green Gables* (New York: Grosset & Dunlap, 1908), 82.
2. Montgomery, *Anne of Green Gables*, 121–122.

Chapter 12 Love Is . . .

1. Thayer's Greek Lexicon, *makrothymeo*, Biblesoft electronic database, 2011.
2. William Arndt, Frederick W. Danker, and Walter Bauer, *A Greek-English Lexicon of the New Testament and Other Early Christian Literature (BDAG)* 3rd ed. (Chicago: University of Chicago Press, 2000), *makrothymeo*.
3. Thayer's Greek Lexicon, *paroxyno*.
4. Arndt, Danker, and Bauer, *A Greek-English Lexicon*, *chrēsteúomai*.
5. Thayer, *chrēsteúomai*.
6. Thayer, *aschēmoneō*.

Chapter 13 How to Lose a Friend in Ten Days

1. C. S. Lewis, *Mere Christianity* (San Francisco: HarperOne, 1952, 1980), 122.
2. John MacArthur, MacArthur New Testament Commentary Series (Book 17) (Chicago: Moody Publishers, 1984), 349.
3. *Dover Books on Literature and Drama, Maxims of La Rochefoucauld*, trans. John Heard Jr (Mineola, NY: Dover Publications, 2006), Kindle Edition.
4. John Donne, *Devotions Upon Emergent Occasions*, ed. Anthony Raspa (New York: Oxford University Press, 1987), 107.

Chapter 14 Time to Grow Up

1. Timothy Keller, *The Meaning of Marriage* (New York: Penguin, 2013), 44.
2. A. T. Robertson and Alfred Plummer, *A Critical and Exegetical Commentary on the First Epistle of St. Paul to the Corinthians*, 2nd ed (Edinburgh: T & T Publishing, 1961), 295.

Chapter 15 The Care and Feeding of Friends

1. David Kinnaman and Gabe Lyons, *unChristian* (Grand Rapids, MI: Baker, 2007), 57.
2. Keith, *Anyway: The Paradoxical Commandments*, (New York: Berkley, 2004), 16.
3. Ernest Hemingway, *Ernest Hemingway Selected Letters 1917–1961*, ed. Carlos Baker (New York: Scribner, 1981), 805.

Chapter 16 How Does Your Garden Grow?

1. Richard Foster, *The Celebration of Discipline*, 25th Anniversary Edition (San Francisco: HarperSanFrancisco, 1978, 1988, 1998), 7.
2. Charles Spurgeon, "Small Things Not to Be Despised," The Charles Spurgeon Sermon Collection, https://www.thekingdomcollective.com/spurgeon/sermon/2601/.

About the Author

Kim Wier is an author, speaker, humor columnist, and radio talk-show host on the country's number one Christian radio station, KSBJ Houston. She is also a Bible teacher and women's ministry director. As someone who brings her own perspective as a wife, mother, and professional, Kim has been sharing the experience of walking in faith with other women for twenty years. She lives in east Texas with her husband. Together, they are proud parents of four adult children and two daughter-in-loves, and grandparents to four granddaughters. Kim shares her passions for connecting women, the Word of God, walking with Christ, and laughter at women's events around the country. She is also the coauthor of *Redeeming the Season: Simple Ideas for a Meaningful and Memorable Christmas* and *Redeeming Halloween: Celebrating without Selling Out*. To learn more about inviting Kim to connect with your group, visit www.kimwier.com.